# Tufts University
Medford, Massachusetts

Written by Emily Chasan

Edited by Adam Burns, Meghan Dowdell,
Kimberly Moore, and Jon Skindzier

Layout by Meryl Sustarsic

Additional contributions by Omid Gohari,
Christina Koshzow, Chris Mason, Joey Rahimi,
and Luke Skurman

ISBN # 1-4274-0150-0
© Copyright 2006 College Prowler
All Rights Reserved
Printed in the U.S.A.
www.collegeprowler.com

Last updated: 03/06/08

**Special Thanks To:** Babs Carryer, Andy Hannah, LaunchCyte, Tim O'Brien, Bob Sehlinger, Thomas Emerson, Andrew Skurman, Barbara Skurman, Bert Mann, Dave Lehman, Daniel Fayock, Chris Babyak, The Donald H. Jones Center for Entrepreneurship, Terry Slease, Jerry McGinnis, Bill Ecenberger, Idie McGinty, Kyle Russell, Jacque Zaremba, Larry Winderbaum, Roland Allen, Jon Reider, Team Evankovich, Lauren Varacalli, Abu Noaman, Mark Exler, Daniel Steinmeyer, Jared Cohon, Gabriela Oates, David Koegler, and Glen Meakem.

**Bounce-Back Team:** Benjamin Cassou, Michele Kligman, and Melissa Auerbach.

CollegeProwler®
5001 Baum Blvd.
Suite 750
Pittsburgh, PA 15213

Phone: 1-800-290-2682
Fax: 1-800-772-4972
E-Mail: info@collegeprowler.com
Web Site: www.collegeprowler.com

# How this all started...

When I was trying to find the perfect college, I used every resource that was available to me. I went online to visit school websites; I talked with my high school guidance counselor; I read book after book; I hired a private counselor. Sure, this was all very helpful, but nothing really told me what life was like at the schools I cared about. These sources weren't giving me enough information to be totally confident in my decision.

In all my research, there were only two ways to get the information I wanted.

The first was to physically visit the campuses and see if things were really how the brochures described them, but this was quite expensive and not always feasible. The second involved a missing ingredient: the students. Actually talking to a few students at those schools gave me a taste of the information that I needed so badly. The problem was that I wanted more but didn't have access to enough people.

In the end, I weighed my options and decided on a school that felt right and had a great academic reputation, but truth be told, the choice was still very much a crapshoot. I had done as much research as any other student, but was I 100 percent positive that I had picked the school of my dreams?

Absolutely not.

My dream in creating *College Prowler* was to build a resource that people can use with confidence. My own college search experience taught me the importance of gaining true insider insight; that's why the majority of this guide is composed of quotes from actual students. After all, shouldn't you hear about a school from the people who know it best?

I hope you enjoy reading this book as much as I've enjoyed putting it together. Tell me what you think when you get a chance. I'd love to hear your college selection stories.

**Luke Skurman**
CEO and Co-Founder
*lukeskurman@collegeprowler.com*

## Welcome to College Prowler®

During the writing of College Prowler's guidebooks, we felt it was critical that our content was unbiased and unaffiliated with any college or university. We think it's important that our readers get honest information and a realistic impression of the student opinions on any campus—that's why if any aspect of a particular school is terrible, we (unlike a campus brochure) intend to publish it. While we do keep an eye out for the occasional extremist—the cheerleader or the cynic—we take pride in letting the students tell it like it is. We strive to create a book that's as representative as possible of each particular campus. Our books cover both the good and the bad, and whether the survey responses point to recurring trends or a variation in opinion, these sentiments are directly and proportionally expressed through our guides.

College Prowler guidebooks are in the hands of students throughout the entire process of their creation. Because you can't make student-written guides without the students, we have students at each campus who help write, randomly survey their peers, edit, layout, and perform accuracy checks on every book that we publish. From the very beginning, student writers gather the most up-to-date stats, facts, and inside information on their colleges. They fill each section with student quotes and summarize the findings in editorial reviews. In addition, each school receives a collection of letter grades (A through F) that reflect student opinion and help to represent contentment, prominence, or satisfaction for each of our 20 specific categories. Just as in grade school, the higher the mark the more content, more prominent, or more satisfied the students are with the particular category.

Once a book is written, additional students serve as editors and check for accuracy even more extensively. Our bounce-back team—a group of randomly selected students who have no involvement with the project—are asked to read over the material in order to help ensure that the book accurately expresses every aspect of the university and its students. This same process is applied to the 200-plus schools College Prowler currently covers. Each book is the result of endless student contributions, hundreds of pages of research and writing, and countless hours of hard work. All of this has led to the creation of a student information network that stretches across the nation to every school that we cover. It's no easy accomplishment, but it's the reason that our guides are such a great resource.

When reading our books and looking at our grades, keep in mind that every college is different and that the students who make up each school are not uniform—as a result, it is important to assess schools on a case-by-case basis. Because it's impossible to summarize an entire school with a single number or description, each book provides a dialogue, not a decision, that's made up of 20 different topics and hundreds of student quotes. In the end, we hope that this guide will serve as a valuable tool in your college selection process. Enjoy!

OMID GOHARI ○ CHRISTINA KOSHZOW ○ CHRIS MASON ○ JOEY RAHIMI ○ LUKE SKURMAN ○
*The College Prowler Team*

# Table of Contents

## Introduction from the Author

One day about four years ago, I stood on Tufts' library roof; as the wind blew over my head, I could clearly see the Boston skyline. I just knew I had to spend the next four years of my life there. Fortunately, the admissions committee agreed with me, and here I am writing to tell you about life on the hill.

By the time I arrived at Tufts, I had been to a lot of other top-tier schools where the people I saw were just like me, and I thought that was great. Tufts was different, however. At Tufts, I saw that college is really about growing into something you aren't yet, and the people at Tufts seemed like the kind of people I wanted to become. Tufts students, on the whole, are smart, funny, and interesting, but most importantly, they are passionate about what they are doing. They get excited enough about a topic to create and teach their own course to freshmen. They plaster the entire campus with posters in hopes that a few more people will find out about their group. They are leaders and thinkers, and together they have managed to create an incredibly dynamic community.

Our former provost, Sol Gittleman, once said that he thinks Tufts has perfected the undergraduate experience. An ideal-sized school of about 5,000 undergrads, Tufts teeters on the fence between being a small New England liberal arts college and a large research institution. It's a city school, with a beautiful suburban campus that is situated on the town line of Medford and Somerville. At Tufts, professors truly focus on their students, and the students take everything they are learning and really try to use it. It is a place where extra-curricular activities are just as important as academics, and the University has as much spirit as one four times its size.

What impressed me most about Tufts was that the school had a sense of humor about itself. In the past 20 years, Tufts has become more competitive and more prestigious than its deans ever expected. There are new buildings everywhere, and Tufts is attracting the most talented students in the world. Still, with school colors that don't quite match, an alma mater that nobody knows, a mascot called Jumbo, and a hill so big that first-years need not worry about the Freshman 15, Tufts has retained the spirit that Nathan Tufts breathed when he vowed to "put a light on the hill" in 1852.

Granted, if you live somewhere for an extended period of time, you're bound to find a blemish or two—like my freshman year bathroom, or the unpredictable weather. Still, the college experience here has never been so appetizing. Now, it is your chance to taste a little bit of the world Tufts has to offer—Jumbo sized.

Emily Chasan, Author
Tufts University

# By the Numbers

## General Information

Tufts University
Medford MA, 02215

**Control:**
Private

**Academic Calendar:**
Semester

**Religious Affiliation:**
None

**Founded:**
1852

**Web Site:**
*www.tufts.edu*

**Main Phone**:
(617) 628-5000

**Admissions Phone:**
(617) 627-3170

## Student Body

**Full-Time
Undergraduates**:
4,938

**Part-Time
Undergraduates**:
44

**Total Male
Undergraduates:**
2,446

**Total Female
Undergraduates:**
2,492

→

# Admissions

**Overall Acceptance Rate:**
29%

**Early Decision
Acceptance Rate:**
45%

**Regular Acceptance Rate:**
27%

**Total Applicants:**
15,294

**Total Acceptances:**
4,095

**Freshman Enrollment:**
1,282

**Yield (% of admitted
students who actually enroll):**
31%

**Early Decision Available?**
Yes

**Early Action Available?**
No

**Early Decision Deadline:**
November 15

**Early Decision Notification:**
December 15

**Regular Decision Deadline:**
January 1

**Regular Decision
Notification:**
April 1

**Must-Reply-By Date:**
May 1

**Transfer Applications
Received:**
788

**Transfer Applications
Accepted:**
108

**Transfer Students Enrolled:**
52

**Transfer Application
Acceptance Rate:**
14%

**Common Application
Accepted?**
Yes

**Supplemental Forms?**
Yes

**Admissions E-Mail:**
admissions.inquiry@ase.
tufts.edu

**Admissions Web Site:**
*admissions.tufts.edu*

**SAT I or ACT Required?**
Either

**SAT I Range
(25th–75th Percentile):**
1340–1480

**SAT I Verbal Range
(25th–75th Percentile):**
670–740

**SAT I Math Range
(25th–75th Percentile):**
670–740

**Freshman Retention Rate:**
95%

**Top 10% of
High School Class:**
74%

**Application Fee:**
$60

## Financial Information

**Tuition:**
$33,906

**Room and Board:**
$9,770

**Books and Supplies:**
$800

**Average Need-Based
Financial Aid Package
(including loans, work-study,
grants, and other sources):**
$27,745

**Students Who Applied
for Financial Aid:**
N/A

**Applicants Who Received Aid:**
78%

**Financial Aid Forms
Deadline:**
February 15

**Financial Aid Phone:**
(617) 627-2000

**Financial Aid E-Mail:**
studentservices@ase.tufts.edu

**Financial Aid Web Site:**
*http://finaid.tufts.edu*

# Academics

The Lowdown On...
## Academics

### Degrees Awarded:
Bachelor's
Post-bachelor's certificate
Master's
Post-master's certificate
Doctorate
First professional

### Most Popular Majors:
12% International Relations
8% Economics
6% Political Science
6% English
6% Psychology

### Undergraduate Schools:
College of Arts and Sciences
School of Engineering

➜

**Full-Time Faculty:**
789

**Average Course Load:**
4 or 5 classes

**Student-to-Faculty Ratio:**
8:1

**Graduation Rates:**
**Four-Year:** 86%
**Five-Year:** N/A
**Six-Year:** 92%

## Special Degree Options

Early Notification Program for acceptance to Tufts School of Medicine

Five-year Bachelor of Arts and Bachelor of Fine Arts degrees from Tufts and School of the Museum of Fine Arts

Five-year Bachelor of Music and Bachelor of Arts or Sciences from Tufts and New England Conservatory of Music

Five-year combined bachelor and master's degree in liberal arts or engineering

Independent study

Nine-year three-degree program with School of Engineering and Tufts School of Medicine

Nine-year three-degree program with School of Engineering and Tufts School of Dental Medicine

ROTC

Six-year bachelor and Master of Arts in Law and Diplomacy (MALD) from Tufts and the Fletcher School of Law and Diplomacy

Study Abroad

## AP Test Score Requirements

Possible credit for scores of 4 or 5 (exceptions in language)

## IB Test Score Requirements

Possible credit for scores of 5, 6 or 7

## Sample Academic Clubs

American Institute of Chemical Engineers (AIChE), American Medical Student Association (Pre-Med), American Society of Civil Engineers (ASCE), Biology Society, Child Development Association, Economics Society, Golden Key Honor Society, Math Club, National Society of Collegiate Scholars (NSCS), Pre-Legal Society, Pre-Veterinary Society, Psychology Society, Public Health at Tufts (PHAT), Society of Women Engineers, Tau Beta Pi, Young Entrepreneurs of Tufts (YET)

## Did You Know?

You can take a class on **anything from bugs to massage therapy** in the Experimental College and get full credit.

You can **create and teach your own class** to freshmen in your junior or senior year.

The most popular class is **Introduction to Yiddish Literature**, taught by former Provost Sol Gittleman.

## Best Places to Study:

Campus Center, President's Lawn (weather permitting), Tisch Library

## Students Speak Out On...
# Academics

**"Classes totally depend on the teachers. Some of the teachers are really great and make class interesting, while others make class boring and hard to follow. Overall, I would say most teachers are pretty good."**

Q "The teachers are one of the best aspects of Tufts because they are so **open and accessible** and willing to help. Upper-level courses are designed to bring students' diversity and range of experiences into the classroom to make the material more tangible and meaningful."

Q "The teachers are all extraordinary. They are some of **the smartest and most articulate people** I have ever known. My Middle East professor served in the Jordanian army, and my economic development professor worked for the World Bank in Southeast Asia. There is no shortage of talent at Tufts."

Q "The teachers and classes at Tufts are truly top-notch. A good portion of the teachers at Tufts have worked in their respective fields for long periods of time, and since Tufts is **just underneath Ivy League status**, they are professionals."

Q "The teachers I had were all **very unique, interesting, and approachable**. If I ever had a problem with anything, it was easy to e-mail them, and they would respond helpfully. Most teachers have high expectations of the kids, but are also very fair. I have no complaints about the teachers at Tufts, although I've heard some of the TAs are annoying. You run into TAs mostly when you have a lab for a class, like science."

Q "Professors are within your reach for extra help, or just to chat. I met a couple mentors in my freshman year alone by just going up and seeing them in their office hours. They're generally very nice people, with the exception of a few. My chemistry professor **throws parties in his own house** every now and then, which is pretty rare for a professor. The best thing Tufts has going for it is the quality of its people, including the professors.""

Q "I chose Tufts because I felt the professors were really awesome. They're caring, and **the students connect with them**. I think mine is the general feeling on the campus."

Q "Tufts has been known for teachers that **really care about students' learning and progress**. They make themselves easily accessible if you want their help, something which I highly recommend, but didn't take advantage of until my senior year."

Q "**The size of the class often determines the level of contact** with professors, but generally, if you make the effort, you'll get to know all your professors. All offer office hours and are usually very accessible; they will always accept a phone call or a student who just drops in for help. For the most part, I've had luck with professors, and that comes from advice from other professors."

Q "I loved them. I was an engineering major, and had a great experience with all of my teachers. I really don't have much exposure to liberal arts teachers, but each department has **totally different faculty**."

Q "It was not really until my junior year that I really liked all of my teachers and began to **form relationships with them**. Once you become comfortable with what you want to do, it is easier to relate to teachers, and to take classes with teachers who you like or have heard good things about."

Q "I've had mostly positive experiences with teachers. **There are duds here and there**, but I've had some life-changing professors, and I still keep in touch with some from past semesters. I found them to be really accessible and concerned for their students' well-being, both academically and personally. I've even had professors invite the entire class over to their houses and cook dinner!"

# The College Prowler Take On...
# Academics

A top-tier school, Tufts has an excellent faculty, and academics that are some of the real newsmakers in modern philosophy, medicine, chemistry, and psychology. Classes are exactly what the students make of them, and for the most part, so are the relationships with faculty. Students generally find Tufts' professors approachable, knowledgeable, and easy-going. Office hours are an excellent time to get to know a professor and find out about research opportunities and possible internships, as well as to get some extra ideas outside of the classroom setting.

As for the classes, there are so many options that each semester starts with a "shopping period." Shopping for classes at Tufts is like shopping for a car. What you choose to take depends strongly on both the subject and the instructor. Some professors are Porsches or convertibles, and of course, there are always a few lemons. Don't be afraid to drop a class during the add-drop period if the professor bores you to tears, because there are plenty of other really exciting professors. With such a top-notch faculty, it's important to talk to friends, upperclassmen, and even other faculty members to figure out what courses and teachers are best suited to your taste. Tufts' professors are really just grown up students, and if you take the opportunity to get to know them outside of class, you will really enhance your college experience.

### The College Prowler® Grade on
### Academics: A

A high Academics grade generally indicates that Professors are knowledgeable, accessible, and genuinely interested in their students' welfare. Other determining factors include class size, how well professors communicate, and whether or not classes are engaging.

# Local Atmosphere

## The Lowdown On...
## Local Atmosphere

**Region:**
Northeast

**City, State:**
Medford, Massachusetts

**Setting:**
Suburban

**Distance from Boston:**
20 minutes

**Distance from NYC:**
3 hours, 30 minutes

**Points of Interest:**
American Repertory Theater
Boston Ballet
Boston Pops
Boston Lyric Opera
Boston Symphony Orchestra
Franklin Park Zoo
Harvard Botanical Museum
Museum of Fine Arts
Museum of Science
New England Aquarium
New England Quilt Museum
Paul Revere House
U.S. Constitution Museum

## Closest Shopping Malls:

CambridgeSide Galleria
100 CambridgeSide Pl.,
Cambridge
(617) 621-8666
*www.cambridgeside
galleria.com*

Copley Place
2 Copley Pl. #100, Boston
(617) 369-5000
*www.simon.com*

Faneuil Hall Marketplace/
Quincy Market
4 S Market St. #5, Boston
(617) 523-1300
*www.faneuilhall
marketplace.com*

Newbury Street
Concentrated area of high-end
shops and art galleries

Shops at Prudential Center
800 Boylston St., Boston
(617) 236-3100

## Major Sports Teams:

Bruins (hockey)
Celtics (basketball)
Patriots (football)
Red Sox (baseball)

## Closest Movie Theaters:

AMC Fenway 13
(617) 424-6266

Loews Theatres Boston
Common
(617) 423-3499

Showcase Cinemas Revere
(781) 286-1660

Somerville Theater
(617) 625-5700

## City Web Sites

*www.boston.com*

*www.bostonglobe.com*

*www.bostonusa.com*

*www.boston-online.com*

*www.allaboutboston.com*

## Did You Know?

**Go to the MIT museum**. It is an interactive, hands-on museum displaying Artificial Intelligence, Hall of Holograms, Mechanical Artwork, and other really incredible exhibits. Best of all, it is only $2 to get in with your student ID.

## 5 Fun Facts about Boston:

• Boston has **over 55 colleges within a five-mile radius**.

• When the school year begins, **the average age in Boston is 26**.

• The Big Dig (*www.masspike.com/bigdig/index.html*) is **the most expensive highway project in U.S. history**—at a cost of more than $1 billion per mile; the city has been building the new underground highway for over 13 years.

• The T is **the first American subway system**, opened in 1898.

• Boston Common was **the first public park in America**.

## Famous Bostonians:

| | |
|---|---|
| Samuel Adams | John F. Kennedy |
| Aerosmith | Jack Lemmon |
| Ben Affleck | Leonard Nimoy |
| F. Lee Bailey | Paul Revere |
| Alexander G. Bell | Donna Summer |
| E.E. Cummings | James Taylor |
| Matt Damon | Sam Waterston |

## Local Slang:

**Beantown** – Boston, denoting the town's celebrity for baked beans.

**Book it** – To get out of some place quickly.

**Bubbla** – Water fountain.

**Chowdahead** – Stupid person.

**Bulkie Roll** – Kaiser roll for a sandwich.

**Hahvahd Sqaah** – Harvard Square, spoken with a local accent.

**Jimmies** – Sprinkles for ice cream.

**Rotary** – A traffic circle.

**Mass-holes** – Boston's bad drivers.

**The T** – The Boston subway system.

**Wicked** – Adverb used to amplify the effect of another adverb i.e. "The Red Sox are wicked good this year!"

### Students Speak Out On...
# Local Atmosphere

"Tufts is like its own little world, but as soon as you hop on the T, the whole city of Boston appears on your doorstep. There are endless restaurants, bars, clubs, shops, historical sites, and museums to visit. It's a college town."

Q "The town itself is **just outside Boston**, and although a little small, it's got some good restaurants, bars, and a couple of theaters. Overall, it's not Boston, and although the city is only 20 minutes away, Tufts students rarely go there, even though the subway makes for an easy trip. Tufts is very campus-centered, and it's tough for students to get away from it sometimes, especially without a car."

Q "Tufts bridges together two towns, Medford and Somerville. If one was to look at a map, it would read: Downtown Boston, Cambridge, Somerville, and then Medford, and as you go further outwards from the Boston area into Massachusetts suburbs, you go towards the New Hampshire border. Tufts is on the border between Medford, a **boring and old-fashioned (yet safe) suburb district**, and Somerville, which has been growing at an exponential rate from an almost slummy area into the new alternative district for college students."

Q "It's the best of both worlds. In Medford, Tufts' campus is **as quiet as any college campus** could probably get. You can also have the excitement of the city, if you choose to."

Q "Medford is a quiet, quaint town. Tufts University is the only university there, but don't worry—**there are hundreds more colleges** about 10 minutes away in Boston."

Q "Tufts is in a small town, and **there's not much to do**, but there are so many universities around! Harvard is the closest, then MIT and Boston College. It is definitely cool to go to their parties. Boston's really nice, and there are lots of stores and places to eat, but I wish it would stay open later!"

Q "Boston is the biggest college town in the country. There are **over 500,000 students in the city**, so there are always things to do and people to meet."

Q "The atmosphere is good. It's not too crazy, and there are some things to do at **Davis Square nearby**. If you get on the subway and ride to the next stop away from the school, you end up in Harvard Square, and there's a lot to do there, with shopping and restaurants."

Q "Medford itself is **a small town** and doesn't have much other than Tufts and its downtown area, Medford Square. Boston's a huge town with a ton of colleges that you can visit, and a city with lots of places to go. Boston's about 15 minutes away through the subway, and it's readily accessible. Harvard and MIT are within 10 minutes' reach, and there's a lot to do in Harvard Square. There aren't many places to stay away from—you're in college, so you might as well experiment with everything."

Q "You are really close to Boston, and that proximity affords you great shopping, museums, bars, clubs, and touristy spots. Medford and Somerville are fine, and all of the merchants and locals that I've dealt with are always really nice. **I would not walk around back alleys late at night** by myself, but short of that, it's fine."

Q "The Tufts campus spans two towns, Medford and Somerville. Medford, which is more towards the uphill side of campus, is quieter, but right along the edge of campus is Boston Avenue. There you'll find **Espresso's, the 'official' Tufts pizza place**, as well as Chinese food, a couple of Italian restaurants, a Dunkin Donuts, a liquor store, a crepe restaurant, and a convenience store, among other things."

## The College Prowler Take On...
# Local Atmosphere

If you are venturing off campus for a night, chances are you'll take the T into Cambridge or Boston—but that doesn't mean that there isn't anything going on in Tufts' hometowns. Whether you pronounce them "Medfuhd and Sumahville" or "Medford and Somerville," Tufts' local areas can be accurately categorized as your basic college towns. On the Medford side, you'll find a few local favorite restaurants (Rose's has the best Chinese around, and Sweet Creams is a tasty favorite with custom-made ice cream flavors), but generally, there is more to do in Somerville's Davis Square. Sometimes called "the Paris of Boston," Davis Square is Somerville's "trendy night spot," though what you'll find there is pretty typical of any college town. You'll find students all over the Square, in Diesel playing pool or sipping a latté, in the Somerville Theater watching second-run flicks at the most affordable prices, and at Denise's/JP Licks where they'll be sampling some of the best ice cream in Boston. Don't forget to grab extra napkins.

Tufts has the advantage of being located just a 15-minute T-ride from the center of a city where there is plenty of nightlife, concerts, and shows to entertain the Tufts student body, as well as those of the other 55 Boston-area schools. Although you won't find as many Tufts students in the city as you will in Medford and Somerville, it can make for much better variety in nightlife and activities. Once you've explored the area, you'll find there really is something for every taste in this varied, college-friendly region.

### The College Prowler® Grade on
### Local
### Atmosphere: A-

A high Local Atmosphere grade indicates that the area surrounding campus is safe and scenic. Other factors include nearby attractions, proximity to other schools, and the town's attitude toward students.

# Safety & Security

The Lowdown On...
## Safety & Security

**Number of TU Police:**
58

**TU Police Phone:**
(617) 627-3030

**Safety Services:**
24-hour emergency response
devices and patrols

Blue-light phones

Controlled dormitory access

Late-night transport/escort
service

Security lighting

## Health Center:

124 Professors Row

(617) 627-3350

*http://ase.tufts.edu/health-services*

Hours: Monday–Friday
8 a.m.–8 p.m.,
Saturday 10:30 a.m.–5 p.m.

## Health Services:

Alcohol and health education
Allergy clinics
Basic medical services
Birth control
Flu shots
Massage therapy
On-site visits
Pharmacy services
Psychiatry

## Did You Know?

The most common offense on campus, other than drug and liquor violations, is burglary. In 1997, Tufts won the **Jean Cleary Safe Campus Award**, given annually to colleges and universities that have demonstrated leadership in improving campus safety.

### Students Speak Out On...
# Safety & Security

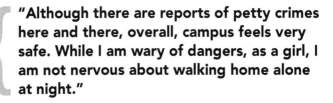

"Although there are reports of petty crimes here and there, overall, campus feels very safe. While I am wary of dangers, as a girl, I am not nervous about walking home alone at night."

Q "Tufts is a very safe place, with a large sense of community and courtesy. **Most security violations come from local residents**. Known as 'townies,' they are not students of the University, but outsiders who come over to the campus on weekends and resent not being able to attend University functions and parties on campus."

Q "I never had an issue with safety, as a man. When they first get to campus, some women are nervous about walking across campus grounds at night, but I have never heard of a criminal incident occurring on campus. **'Townies' sometimes cause trouble at house or frat parties**, but rarely cause any trouble outside of that. I've heard of a couple of shouting matches and low-key brawls between guys from town and students, but nothing that would prevent me from feeling safe."

Q "I have never felt unsafe, even late at night. The campus police offer **a self defense class for girls**, and have made many efforts to remind students that they aren't always as safe in the 'real world' as they are on campus. It's easy to take our safety for granted."

Q "I'm from New York City, so I feel really safe. You can't be anywhere on campus without being able to sprint to **a dorm phone or a blue-light emergency phone** because they're never more than maybe 100 yards away. We have a police station on campus called the TUPD that are always open."

Q "To my knowledge, there hasn't been a major safety dilemma at Tufts since I have been enrolled, so security must be pretty good. There are many blue-light telephones and **the campus is well lit**, so I have never felt unsafe walking around on campus by myself at night."

Q "The working-class neighborhoods that surround Tufts give access to townies that commit minor thefts, and there is an occasional broken window. But if doors are locked at night, there is never a problem, especially in the college dormitories where **townies have no access**."

Q "Safety is not an issue. Campus is totally safe to walk around at night. I had a job off campus the first semester of my freshman year, and I felt fine walking home at night. **Dorms are always locked, but entrance is easy**. That may seem a bit unsafe, but it's never been a problem. In fact, you'll find that it's much nicer to have easy access to dorms, and not have restrictions on who can stay over like at other schools. I feel totally safe at Tufts, and in Boston, for that matter."

### The College Prowler Take On...
# Safety & Security

Tufts has gone to incredible lengths to make students feel safe on campus. With safety services like TEMS, police escorts, and a strong police presence, Tufts students feel safe walking around their well-monitored, well-lit campus, even at night. Don't let the "you can't spell stupid without TUPD" jokes fool you—TUPD officers are always around campus, and willing to help out in any way they can. Every year, there are a few assaults, robberies, and hate crimes, but rarely are they committed by Tufts students or members of the Tufts community.

There are blue-light safety phones all over campus, and Tufts also has a fire department and an emergency medical service (TEMS) on hand. Every dorm has its own unique key, and the ResLife office is currently phasing in infrared electronic keys for added security. Above all else, "townies" present the biggest threat around the Tufts area, and even this isn't worth getting your panties in a bunch. Many townies are friendly and show respect towards Tufts students, but students may encounter a curmudgeon every once in a while. If you feel threatened by such an individual, feel free to beat him or her on the head with the largest textbook on hand!

**B+**

The College Prowler® Grade on

Safety & Security: B+

A high grade in Safety & Security means that students generally feel safe, campus police are visible, blue light phones and escort services are readily available, and safety precautions are not overly necessary.

# Computers

The Lowdown On...
## Computers

**High-Speed Network?**
Yes

**Wireless Network?**
Yes

**Number of Labs:**
2 public labs

**24-Hour Labs:**
None

**Charge to Print?**
Yes, 10 cents per page

**Number of Computers:**
2,008

**Operating Systems:**
Linux
Mac OS
Windows

### Computing Center at Eaton Hall

This is the main campus computer lab. It has all the latest software, and over 150 computers.

### Halligan Hall

This is the computer science laboratory. Computers are Linux-based, and there are similar computers at the Engineering Project Development Center in Anderson Hall.

### Instructional Labs

Braker 002 and Eaton 208 are two computer labs reserved for instructional use for classes only, which professors must sign up for.

### Mugar Hall

This lab is in the Fletcher School, and only graduate students are allowed to use it, unless all other labs are closed. There are additional computers available for use at the library, and there are instructional labs that professors can reserve in Eaton Hall and Braker Hall.

---

### Did You Know?

Tufts University offers **discounted prices for Dell, IBM, and Apple computers** when purchased through the University.

### Students Speak Out On...
# Computers

> "The network is fast. It's usually expected that you would have your own computer. But the labs are available, and they are open long hours for students who may need them."

Q "Computing on campus is really good. **The main lab is really big**, and there are usually enough computers to go around. Many buildings on campus also have wireless Internet, so that's a good perk to bring a laptop. Everyone has their own computers, so the lab is just a good place to go to kill time mid-day, or do that last-minute paper in a less distracting environment."

Q "Those students without their own computer will probably be at **more of a social loss than an academic one**. The Tufts campus is split into uphill and downhill sections that are difficult to walk across on a whim. Plans are therefore usually made beforehand. Because every dorm room is set up with a T1 Internet LAN connection, which lets your computer be on the Internet at fast speeds day and night, many students leave their computers on all day and all night. Plans are often made using chat programs such as AOL Instant Messenger, or by phone."

Q "**I can't imagine not having your own computer**. The main lab here is fairly large, but a lot of coursework is online. Also, don't forget all the writing that needs to be done for most courses. The computer lab just becomes impractical. Also, they have instituted a pay-for-printing policy, which means every page you print will cost you a dime. That could add up."

**Q** "The computer network is really fast. But **be careful about getting caught using KaZaA**. The computer labs are also good. They have plenty of computers, and they are rarely full. You should definitely bring a computer if you have one. It's so much more convenient."

**Q** "Computer access can be problematic at times. The labs are great if you go early, but you have to know when to use them. During midterms and finals you need to get to the lab five minutes before opening (8 a.m.) to get a computer. I'd say **your best bet is to bring a laptop**."

**Q** "I would suggest bringing your own computer. The labs are not really near the dorms, so you have to walk in the snow or rain. But, **they usually aren't that crowded**. I've never gone there and not been able to sit down immediately."

**Q** "It's more convenient to bring a computer, but **you definitely don't have to**. The computer labs only get crowded around finals time, so you can always find one to use, and, in a pinch, you can usually borrow one from a roommate or someone on your hall. It's nice to have one for IM and e-mail, though."

# The College Prowler Take On...
# Computers

Tufts is a well-wired campus, and students don't complain about access to computer labs or the Internet connection from their dorm rooms. Over 80 percent of Tufts students bring their own computers to campus, and the campus is completely wired. There is a huge social element to computers at Tufts. Just as many students use AOL Instant Messenger for all of their communication needs, as they do the telephone. There are three main computer labs in addition to computers in the library, though Eaton is the main computing center with two floors and over 260 computers. Students have recently enjoyed new, longer hours at the computer lab, but are quick to complain about the new printing charges (10 cents per page).

Tufts is not specifically a Mac or a PC campus, and both operating systems are compatible with anything you'll need for class. The library and the Campus Center have wireless Internet ports as well, so a laptop is probably your best bet if you want to take advantage of portability; plenty of students choose desktops, however. Though you can certainly survive without one, you'll be at a social (and potentially academic) disadvantage at Tufts without your own computer.

**B**

The College Prowler® Grade on

Computers: B

A high grade in Computers designates that computer labs are available, the computer network is easily accessible, and the campus' computing technology is up to date.

# Facilities

**The Lowdown On...**
## Facilities

**Student Center:**
The Mayer Campus Center

**Athletic Center:**
Ames Human Performance
Center
Cousens Gymnasium
Gantcher Center
Hamilton Pool

**Libraries:**
Tisch is the main library; there
are five other department
libraries located on campus

**Campus Size:**
150 acres

**Popular Places to Chill:**
Brown & Brew
The Campus Center
Dorm common rooms
The President's Lawn

## What Is There to Do on Campus?

The a cappella scene at Tufts is huge, and you'll see postings for shows for one or a few of the University's six groups throughout the semester. They kick off the year with the Orientation Show the night after students arrive back on campus in the fall.

Tufts' seasonal carnivals draw many new activities to the campus. There are all types of events going on in the Campus Center on these nights.

Poetry readings and solo guitar acts are also popular fare around campus. The Concert Board hand picks musicians to come play at Tufts. There is usually a fall rock show, winter jazz show, and "Spring Fling."

The end-of-the-semester dance shows by Tufts Dance Collective and Spirit of Color are generally packed to the capacity of the auditorium. Here, you have a good chance to see all your fellow students "shake it around."

Check out free weekly films offered in Barnum Hall.

Every Friday night, Hotung Café has music and dancing, but you're more likely to see the crowds there on a Thursday night for local bands.

In addition to the drama department, there are several student-run theater groups on campus, so Tufts' stages never remain empty for long. Each group produces major and minor productions, so keep your eyes peeled.

## Movie Theater on Campus?

Film Series offers weekly movie showings

## Bowling on Campus?

No

## Bar on Campus?

Yes, Hotung Café

## Coffeehouse on Campus?

Yes, Brown & Brew in Curtis Hall, and the Rez in the
Campus Center

## Favorite Things to Do on Campus

Chill with friends in a dorm room, grab a coffee at Brown &
Brew, check out a play or movie on campus, or watch an a
cappella show

Students Speak Out On...
# Facilities

{ **"Facilities are nice and modern. The gym is one of the best around, but the Campus Center can get overcrowded. It would be nice to have a larger community space."**

Q "The computer labs have up-to-date, fast computers. The Campus Center is **a chill place for people to hang out** and get some food."

Q "**Some of the facilities are a little on the older, 1970s side**, but there are rarely complaints. The athletics facility is new, but too small—in fact, many facilities are a little on the small side, with not quite enough space to deal with all the students. But I guess that happens at any college."

Q "The Campus Center is pretty cool. It's a good place for people to meet up, and there are a bunch of little study nooks, and a couple big screen TVs (with cable) located upstairs. The library is nice with its **cozy armchairs**, but students beware, for they are known to lull studiers to sleep!"

Q "We have a gym with good equipment, but I honestly think that it could be much better. The student center has **good food, a pool table, a Ping-Pong table**, a TV, three floors, a small club, and study areas. It's pretty nice."

Q "The facilities on campus are great. The athletic facilities are wonderful, and we have **good foreign language labs**. The student center isn't that big, but there are a couple of areas where they have some big TVs and lots of couches. You can even get discounted tickets for movies and stuff."

Q "I love the Campus Center and our athletic facilities. We have **a new track**, and we get new weight equipment every year. Timing for the gym is important because crowds come in during the afternoon."

Q "**The gym is a lot nicer than at most other colleges**, and has become very popular. It's probably your best chance to see someone socially, but all the academic facilities are good."

Q "Some of the older places, like **the Campus Center, could use renovations**, but the Mugar computer lab was remodeled recently, as well as Ginn Library, and a new athletic facility opened up, as well. It's big enough to house an indoor track and tennis courts, and the school holds a lot of big functions there. We get speakers like Bill Clinton, Madeline Albright, Al Gore, and Colin Powell."

Q "We have new athletic and computer facilities. Our student center is really nice, and there is talk of expanding it. We have **a new, gorgeous library**, and the Student Services Center is pretty new, as well."

## The College Prowler Take On...
# Facilities

Tufts takes a lot of pride in its campus buildings and facilities, and they are always well kept and well maintained. There has been a flurry of construction over the last 10 years with more new buildings and renovations every year. Still, students who wish that Tufts could compete with the facilities at larger, more well-endowed schools can always find room to complain.

Generally, students complain that the buildings are a little too small. There are minor problems with overcrowding, but with such a small student body, this is only noticeable during busy times. Some of the recent additions like Dowling Hall and the Tisch Library have greatly improved students' quality of life. There is something new on campus every fall, and Tufts is steadily trying to keep up with the growing needs of the student body. As far as meeting these needs, the school has come close, but hasn't quite hit the mark yet. A water park on campus wouldn't hurt.

**B**

The College Prowler® Grade on

**Facilities: B**

A high Facilities grade indicates that the campus is aesthetically pleasing and well maintained, facilities are state-of-the-art, and libraries are exceptional. Other determining factors include the quality of both athletic and student centers and an abundance of things to do on campus.

# Campus Dining

The Lowdown On...
## Campus Dining

**Freshman Meal Plan Requirement?**
Yes

**Meal Plan Average Cost:**
$2,285

**Places to Grab a Bite with Your Meal Plan:**

**Brown & Brew**
Food: Coffee, sandwiches, pastries, sushi
Location: Curtis Hall
Hours: Monday–Friday 8 a.m.–1 a.m., Saturday–Sunday 12 p.m.–1 a.m.

### Carmichael Dining Hall

Food: All-you-can-eat, salad bar, pizza, grill, vegetarian

Location: Uphill, basement floor of Carmichael Hall

Hours: Monday–Thursday 7:15 a.m.–8 p.m., Friday 7:15 a.m.–7:30 p.m., Saturday 8 a.m.–7:30 p.m., Sunday 11 a.m.–8 p.m.

### Commons

Food: Sandwiches, grill, soup, salad bar, sushi

Location: Campus Center

Hours: Monday–Thursday 8 a.m.–8 p.m., Friday 8 a.m.–2 p.m., Saturday closed, Sunday 10 a.m.– 12 a.m.

### Dewick-MacPhie Dining Hall

Food: All-you-can-eat salad bar, pizza, grill, vegetarian, breakfast buffet including belgian waffles

Location: Across from the Campus Center

Hours: Monday-Thursday 7:15 a.m.–8 p.m., Friday 7:15 a.m.–7:30 p.m., Saturday 8 a.m.–7:30 p.m., Sunday 11 a.m.–8 p.m.

### Hodgdon Good-To-Go

Food: Take-out, Chinese, Mexican, sandwiches, hot dogs, breakfasts

Location: Hodgdon Hall basement

Hours: Monday–Thursday 8 a.m.–10 p.m., Friday 8 a.m.–4 p.m

### Hotung Café

Food: Italian-style; pizza and calzones

Location: Campus Center

Hours: Monday–Friday 11:30 a.m.–12 a.m., Saturday–Sunday and Holidays 2 p.m.–12 a.m.

### Jumbo Express

Food: Grocery store

Location: Campus Center

Hours: Monday–Friday 10 p.m.–12 a.m., Saturday– Sunday 1 p.m.–12 a.m.

### Mulger Café

Location: Mugar Hall

Food: Coffee, bagels, pastries, hot food bar, salads, sandwiches, sushi

Hours: Monday–Thursday 8 p.m.–7 p.m., Friday 8 a.m.–2 p.m.

### Oxfam Café

Food: Vegan, vegetarian

Location: Miller Hall Basement

Hours: Monday–Thursday 10:30 a.m.–12 a.m., Friday 10:30 a.m.–4:30 p.m., 10 p.m.–1 a.m., Sunday 6:30 p.m.–12 a.m.

### The Rez

Food: Drinks, coffee, muffins, danishes, snacks

Location: Campus Center

Hours: Monday–Wednesday 8:30 a.m.–12:30 a.m., Thursday 8:30 a.m.– 11 p.m., Friday 8:30 a.m.– 6 p.m., Saturday 12 p.m.– 6 p.m., Sunday 12 p.m.– 12:30 a.m.

### Tab Eatery

Food: Homemade soup, sandwiches, salads, snacks

Location: Administration Building

Hours: Monday–Friday 8 a.m.–2 p.m.

### Tower Café

Food: Fair Trade coffee, tea, fresh juice, sushi, sandwiches, snacks, pastries

Location: Tisch Library

Hours: Sunday–Thursday, 12 p.m.–1 a.m., Friday– Saturday 12 p.m.–7 p.m.

## 24-Hour On-Campus Eating?

No

## Student Favorites:

Brown & Brew

Commons

Dewick-MacPhie

## Off-Campus Places to Use Your Meal Plan:

Andrea's House of Pizza (781) 391-9093

Domino's Pizza (617) 629-0444

Espresso Pizzeria (781) 396-0062

Panda Palace (781) 396-8881

Pasta Pisa/Café de Crepe (781) 391-2030

Wing Works (617) 666-9000

## Did You Know?

**Dewick and MacPhie** used to be separate dining halls.

Tufts Dining Services was **once ranked second best** (in regards to food selection) in the nation.

"Points" are the same as "Dining Dollars," only better, because **you can get MOPS delivery** with them.

**Profits from the volunteer-run Oxfam Café are donated** to an organization that funds self-development and disaster-relief projects all over the world. The Café is also in cahoots with the Oxfam Collective, a campus organization involved in hunger-related issues.

## Other Options

MOPS (Meals on Points) allows you to get food delivered to your room from selected MOPS vendors, and everything but the tip comes off your meal plan. Students just call any of the off-campus restaurants accepting the Tufts meal plan. Careful though—MOPS only works for delivery.

## Students Speak Out On...
# Campus Dining

**"We have awesome food. My parents were shocked. I swear the food is better than home cooked."**

Q "Food on campus is good for mass-produced cafeteria food. People complain about the tedium of it, and many sophomores **order in on Points** instead of going to the dining halls. On campus, the Brown & Brew is a popular coffee and late-night study place, which closes at 1 a.m. There's also a campus food mart, and the Campus Center has two different cafeteria-type places that accept cash and Points."

Q "The food here is so good! Tufts food is ranked second best in the country, I think. **It's a little tough to ward off the Freshman 15**, but it's worth it! There are two cafeterias on campus, a take-out place, and a Campus Center that only takes cash."

Q "The **food on campus is surprisingly good**. The Campus Center is the best place to eat, and Brown & Brew is pretty good, too. Most people like the dining halls, but after freshman year, you probably won't go to the dining halls as often."

Q "I must say that, as a first-year student, **I was very impressed with the food** because of the wide variety of freshly grilled meat, and salads. But after a year of not being able to eat home cooking, you get kind of frustrated with the food.

Q "**I suggest eating at Dewick-MacPhie Hall** because they have a better selection, but sometimes Carmichael Hall has its ups. The Commons, which is located in the Campus Center, is also good if you like sandwiches and such. There are also options in meal plans to get Points for off-campus spots."

Q "Tufts has excellent food, though like anything, **you get sick of it after a year**. There are two big dining halls, some other smaller ones, a deli in the Campus Center, a dedicated vegan place, a café, and some small spots tucked into the graduate school buildings."

Q "During your freshman year, you are roped into getting the unlimited meal plan. **Every freshman has to get it**. At some institutions, it would be worth complaining, but the dining hall food is so good at Tufts that it's nice to have."

Q "**They try to meet every student's needs**, and they do a good job at it. The required purchase of an unlimited meal plan for freshmen is a bummer because not that many people will actually use up any more than half of the 400 meals given a semester!"

Q "I found the food to be disgusting. **You will be ordering in all the time**."

Q "**The food is nothing spectacular**, although I have been to other places and their food stinks, so I guess that's a sign that Tufts' food is good. There's plenty of variety."

Q "Apparently, we have good food in the two dining halls on campus. I'm sick of dining hall food, but the dining halls **provide a great atmosphere** for first year when you get to know everyone."

Q "Dining halls are for freshmen and sophomores. Once you get to be an upperclassman, you usually eat at the Campus Center, which **I love as much as the cafeterias**. There's plenty of selection, and a huge salad bar."

Q "The food is said to be **better than most other schools**, and I would say it's alright. There is a large selection in the dining halls, but we also have a service that delivers food from restaurants in the area. The deliveries don't offer such a great selection, but they are more for juniors and seniors, who usually make their own food anyway."

Q "The food is amazingly good for college dining services, but of course, it can get repetitive. You just have to **get a little more creative**!"

# The College Prowler Take On...
# Campus Dining

The verdict is out. The majority of Tufts students will tell you that the food on campus is great. Students here who have been to other university cafeterias agree that they are lucky, because it could have been a lot worse. There are always fresh vegetables and fruits in the dining halls, Campus Center eateries are generally packed, and Sunday brunch is one of the largest social events on campus. The one drawback is that the food can get monotonous after a while, but fortunately, the MOPS program provides an opportunity to get a different flavor and order in, while still putting the bill on your meal plan.

The unlimited meal plan is required for the first year, which some students resent. It is true that you probably won't get to eat all the food you pay for before the end of the semester. However, this does provide a common bond between you and everyone in your freshman class having the same meal plan, and remember, there are still three more years to experience all the on-campus options outside of the dining hall, like Brown & Brew and Dewick.

### The College Prowler® Grade on
### Campus Dining: A-

Our grade on Campus Dining addresses the quality of both school-owned dining halls and independent on campus restaurants as well as the price, availability, and variety of food available.

# Off-Campus Dining

The Lowdown On...
## Off-Campus Dining

### Restaurant Prowler: Popular Places to Eat!

#### Anna's Taqueria
Food: Mexican
236A Elm St., Davis Square, Somerville
(617) 666-3900
Cool Features: Good, fast, and dirt-cheap authentic burritos.
Price: $2–$5
Hours: Daily 10 a.m.–11 p.m.

#### Antonia's Italian Bistro
Food: Italian
37 Davis Sq., Somerville
(617) 623-6700
Cool Features: 20 percent discount on take-out orders with student ID.
Price: $6–$15
Hours: Daily 10 a.m.–11 p.m.

#### Blue Shirt Café
Food: Gourmet wraps, breakfast, smoothies
424 Highland Ave., Somerville

### (Blue Shirt Café, continued)

(617) 629-7641

Cool Features: Juice bar.

Price: $4–$6

Hours: Sunday–Wednesday 8 a.m.–9 p.m., Thursday–Saturday 8 a.m.–10 p.m.

### Café de Crepe

Food: Crepes, coffee

283 Boston Ave., Medford

(781) 391-2030

Cool Features: Delivers, so you can have crepes in bed!

Price: $5–$8

Hours: Saturday–Thursday 11 a.m.–11 p.m., Friday 4 p.m.–11 p.m.

### Diva Indian Bistro

Food: Indian

246 Elm St., Somerville

(617) 629-4963

Cool Features: Cool bar.

Price: $8–$21

Hours: Daily 11:30 a.m.–11 p.m.

### Espresso Pizza

Food: American

336 Boston Ave., Medford

(781) 396-0062

Cool Features: Great ice cream.

Price: $5–$12

Hours: Monday–Wednesday 11:30 a.m.–12:30 a.m., Thursday 11:30 a.m.–1 a.m.

### (Espresso Pizza, continued)

Friday–Saturday 11:30 a.m.–2 a.m.

### Fusion Express

Food: Thai

195 Elm St., Somerville

(617) 623-3354

Cool Features: Green tea, coconut ice cream, pad Thai

Price: $8–$15

Hours: Monday–Saturday 10:30 a.m.–10:30 p.m., Sunday 4:30 p.m.–10:30 p.m.

### Golden Light

Food: Chinese

24 College Ave., Somerville

(617) 666-9822

Cool Features: Open late.

Price: $6–$10

Hours: Sunday–Thursday 4:30 p.m.–2 a.m., Friday–Saturday 4:30 p.m.–3 a.m.

### Joshua Tree Bar & Grill

Food: American, Italian, Mexican

256 Elm St., Somerville

(617) 623-9910

*www.joshuatreebarandgrill.com*

Cool Features: Lobster specials. Dinner and movie Sunday nights 9–11 p.m.

Price: $7–$20

Hours: Sunday–Friday 11:30 a.m.–1 a.m., Sunday 10:30 a.m.–1 a.m.

### Panda Palace

Food: Chinese

442 Salem St., Medford

(781) 396-8881

Cool Features: MOPS delivery, all-you-can-eat buffet.

Price: $6–$14

Hours: Sunday–Thursday 11:30 a.m.–10 p.m., Friday–Saturday 11:30 a.m.–11 p.m.

### Picante Mexican Grill

Food: Mexican

217 Elm St., Davis Square, Somerville

(617) 628-6394

Cool Features: Biggest burritos.

Price: $4–$9

Hours: Monday–Friday 11 a.m.–10:30 p.m., Saturday 10 a.m.–11 p.m., Sunday 10 a.m.–10 p.m.

### Rose's Chinese Restaurant

Food: Chinese, sushi

321 Boston Ave., Medford

(781) 395-8885

Cool Features: Healthy and low-calorie dishes.

Price: $5–$33

Hours: Monday–Saturday 11 a.m.–11 p.m., Sunday 3 p.m.–11 p.m.

### SoundBites

Food: Breakfast, Middle Eastern

708 Broadway Ave., Ball Square, Somerville

(617) 623-8338

Cool Features: Take out.

Price: $5–$8

Hours: Daily 7 a.m.–3 p.m.

### Tasty Gourmet

Food: Deli

321B Boston Ave., Medford

(781) 391-9969

Cool Features: Gourmet sandwiches—try the Stuffed Pilgrim!

Price: $5–$8

Hours: Monday–Saturday 7 a.m.–9 p.m., Sunday 7 a.m.–6 p.m.

### Wing Works

Food: American

201 Elm St., Davis Square, Somerville

(617) 666-9000

Cool Features: "Where fine dining meets heat-n-eat."

Price: $6–$11

Hours: Monday–Thursday 11 a.m.–11 p.m., Friday–Saturday 11 a.m.–12 a.m., Sunday 12 p.m.–10 p.m.

### Yoshi's

Food: Japanese, sushi

132 College Ave.,
Powderhouse Square,
Somerville

(617) 623-9263

Cool Features: Awesome
miso soup.

Price: $5–$28

Hours: Monday–Thursday
5 p.m.–10:30 p.m., Friday–
Saturday 5 p.m.–11 p.m.,
Sunday 5 p.m.–10 p.m.

## Other Places to Check Out:

Denise's Homemade Ice Cream

J P Licks

Nick's House of Pizza

Sweet Creams

## Closest Grocery Stores:

Star Market
49 White Street, Porter Square
Shopping Center, Cambridge
(617) 876-1450

Johnnie's FoodMaster
105 Alewife Brook Parkway,
Somerville
(617) 660-1342

Store 24 (convenience store)
133 Main St., Medford
(781) 395-1047

## Best Pizza:

Espresso Pizza

## Best Chinese:

Rose's

## Best Breakfast:

SoundBites

## Best Wings:

Wing Works

## Best Healthy:

Blue Shirt Café

## Best Place to Take Your Parents:

Diva

## Student Favorites:

Anna's Taqueria

Rose's

SoundBites

Yoshi's

### Students Speak Out On...
# Off-Campus Dining

> **"The take-out places like Espresso's are pretty decent. If you venture into Davis Square, there are some nice restaurants like the Joshua Tree or sandwich places like Blue Shirt Café."**

Q "The restaurants off campus are pretty good. If you want to stay close to campus, **Tasty Gourmet is really good**. Then there are some good places in Davis Square and Porter Square. If you want cheap decent food, Espressos is good. Try to stay away from cheap Chinese food."

Q "In Davis, there are a couple great Indian food places, and **Anna's Taqueria is a must-go**. They serve the best burritos in town for less than four dollars, and their salsa is extraordinarily good."

Q "**The restaurants off campus are good**, and in Boston they're amazing. The standard ordering places are pretty good—but in Davis, there's a crepe place that I adore, an awesome old-school diner, and a bunch of other nice places with meals from five to twenty dollars."

Q "The off-campus restaurants are the highlight of Tufts. We have some incredible food. SoundBites offers delicious breakfast brunches. Rose's Chinese Restaurant offers incredible Chinese. Anna's Taqueria and Mexican Picante both offer Mexican food to die for, and **Diva offers an incredible taste of Indian cuisine**. There is a heavy Asian influence in the area, as well, besides the usual Chinese take out. Asian options include many fine Thai and Vietnamese restaurants, as well as French Cambodian options."

Q "**There are many Irish pubs**, and if you are in the mood for the unusual, downtown Boston holds many exotic options such as Ethiopian and Moroccan Cuisine. There is a general consensus around campus that Boston and the surrounding area are home to a million and one restaurants."

Q "If you like Chinese, **Rose's and Panda Palace** are really good—at least better than the other Chinese spots. Anna's Taqueria is also good if you like Mexican. It's really close to Tufts, and it's cheap."

Q "There are great surrounding take out places— **Espresso's Pizza is my personal favorite**. We have the usual cluster of delivery spots, and the Tufts' meal plan you have to buy comes with 'points' that are good for delivery at three or four restaurants, which is useful for when you don't feel like walking."

Q "There are some good restaurants right near campus. There is one very popular pizza place, Espresso's, which also sells subs and other foods. There are a handful of decent Asian food places, and one really good one called Rose's. Of course, if you go into Boston, or even Cambridge with Harvard and MIT, there are **endless wonderful restaurants**."

Q "There are some decent places in Medford, but no really nice places—**it's kind of a crappy town for restaurants**. The good places are not on the meal plan, so you have to pay for them—which is inconvenient and expensive."

Q "There are no on-campus restaurants, but Boston Avenue (with Espresso's, Nick's, and Tasty) is a short walk away. They are big on college food—pizza, Mexican, and sandwiches. But if you want fancier stuff, **Boston is not that far away**. You can also visit Davis Square by Tufts' shuttle, and there are a lot of good restaurants there, like Joshua Tree, which is one of my favorites."

### The College Prowler Take On...
# Off-Campus Dining

Dining off campus can be a great way to bring a little more excitement into your diet, and it's also a great way to explore the local communities. There are some restaurants already affiliated with Tufts on the MOPS program, and Medford and Somerville have some excellent dining options. If you want to trek a little further, Harvard Square and surrounding Boston, particularly the North End, are full of hundreds of different kinds of foods and local specialties.

Students will often go out to big dinners, lunches, or brunches at local restaurants. You have to be careful, though, because going out to dinner a lot can get expensive, so make sure to limit dining out to special occasions. Not to worry, though, "settling" for Tufts on-campus eating options certainly does not spell out d-o-o-m for anyone.

**The College Prowler® Grade on**

## Off-Campus Dining: A

A high Off-Campus Dining grade implies that off campus restaurants are affordable, accessible, and worth visiting. Other factors include the variety of cuisine and the availability of alternative options (vegetarian, vegan, kosher, etc.).

# Campus Housing

The Lowdown On...
## Campus Housing

### Room Types:
Doubles, singles, triples, as well as 2-, 3-, 4-, 6-, and 10-person apartment-style suites (with common room, bathroom, bedrooms, some with kitchens)

### Best Dorms:
Hillside Apartments
Miller
South
West

### Worst Dorms:
Haskell
Wren

### Undergrads Living on Campus:
75%

### Number of Dormitories:
24

# Dormitories:

### 9-11 Sunset Avenue

Floors: 2

Total Occupancy: 6

Bathrooms: Shared by suite/floor

Coed: Yes, single-sex by suite

Residents: Upperclassmen

Room Types: Three-person suites with single rooms

Special Features: Each floor has its own bathroom, kitchen, and living room.

### 10 Winthrop Street

Floors: 2

Total Occupancy: 6

Bathrooms: Shared by suite/floor

Coed: Yes, single-sex by suite

Residents: Upperclassmen

Room Types: Three-person suites with single rooms

Special Features: Each floor has its own bathroom and kitchen, two first-floor living rooms.

### 12 Dearborn Road

Floors: 3

Total Occupancy: 15

Bathrooms: Two shared by house

Coed: Yes

Residents: Upperclassmen

Room Types: Singles, doubles

Special Features: Furnished, common room, kitchen, laundry.

### 90-94 Curtis Street

Floors: 3

Total Occupancy: 18

Bathrooms: Shared by suite/floor

Coed: Yes

Residents: Upperclassmen

Room Types: Four- and six-person suites with varying single and double bedrooms

Special Features: Each floor has its own bathroom, kitchen, and living room (some have two living rooms), storage spaces, each room is different.

### 176 Curtis Street

Floors: 3

Total Occupancy: 8

Bathrooms: Two shared by house

Coed: Yes, second and third floors are all female

Residents: Upperclassmen

Room Types: Four singles, three two-person apartments

Special Features: Furnished, common kitchen, laundry.

### Bush Hall

Floors: 4

Total Occupancy: 114

Bathrooms: Eight single-sex bathrooms per floor shared by four to six students

Coed: Yes

Residents: Mostly freshmen and sophomores

Room Types: Three singles, doubles

### (Bush Hall, continued)

Special Features: Common room, study lounges, first floor kitchen, bike storage, laundry, vending machines.

### Carmichael Hall

Floors: 5

Total Occupancy: 257

Bathrooms: Two single-sex bathrooms and shower rooms (four showers each) per floor (but none on the fifth floor)

Coed: Yes, by wing on the first three floors, floors four and five are all female

Residents: Mostly freshmen and sophomores; some juniors

Room Types: Singles, doubles, five triples

Special Features: Carmichael dining hall, first floor is Healthy Living, common room, study lounges, bike storage, laundry, vending machines, surrounds courtyard (the green).

### Carpenter House

Floors: 3

Total Occupancy: 40

Bathrooms: Shared by floor

Coed: Yes, floor two is all female, and floor three is all male

Residents: Upperclassmen

Room Types: Singles, doubles, one triple

Special Features: Common room, two single-sex floors, kitchen, Ping-Pong table, laundry.

### Haskell Hall

Floors: 4 + basement

Total Occupancy: 148

Bathrooms: Shared by suite (two showers, toilets, and sinks each)

Coed: Yes, single-sex by suite

Residents: Mostly freshmen and sophomores; some juniors

Room Types: 10-person suites (four doubles, two singles)

Special Features: Common room, study lounges, kitchen, bike storage, laundry, vending machines.

### Hill Hall

Floors: 5

Total Occupancy: 164

Bathrooms: Shared by floor (except fifth floor)

Coed: Yes

Residents: Freshmen and sophomores

Room Types: Singles, doubles, one three-person apartment

Special Features: Mail services, aerobics studio, floors three, four, and five are Healthy Living, common room, study lounges, second floor kitchen, bike storage, laundry, vending machines.

### Hillside Apartments

Floors: 5 + basement

Total Occupancy: 216

Bathrooms: Shared by suite

Coed: Yes

Residents: Upperclassmen

### (Hillside Apartments, continued)

Room Types: Six-person suites, ten-person suites

Special Features: Apartment-style, common room, study lounges, kitchens, laundry, vending machines, parking lot.

### Hodgdon Hall

Floors: 3 + basement

Total Occupancy: 155

Bathrooms: Shared by floor or wing

Coed: Yes, single-sex by floor

Residents: Mostly freshmen and sophomores; some juniors

Room Types: Singles, doubles, one two-person apartment

Special Features: Hodgdon Take-It-Away, common room, study lounges, two kitchens, bike storage, laundry, vending machines.

### Houston Hall

Floors: 3 + basement

Total Occupancy: 260

Bathrooms: Four single-sex bathrooms shared by floor

Coed: Yes, single-sex by room

Residents: Freshmen

Room Types: Doubles, one four-person apartment (two double bedrooms)

Special Features: Common room, study lounges, Ping-Pong and air hockey tables, a TV, kitchen, bike storage, laundry, vending machines, Scholar-in-Residence, surrounds courtyard (the Green).

### Latin Way

Floors: 4

Total Occupancy: 216

Bathrooms: Shared by suite

Coed: Yes, single-sex by suite

Residents: Upperclassmen

Room Types: Four-person suites

Special Features: Apartment-style, common room, study lounges, kitchens, laundry, vending machines.

### Lewis Hall

Floors: 4

Total Occupancy: 219

Bathrooms: Four single-sex bathrooms shared by floor

Coed: Yes, single-sex by suite

Residents: Freshmen and sophomores

Room Types: Singles, doubles, three triples, one four-person and two two-person apartments

Special Features: Crafts Center, common room, study lounges, first floor kitchen, bike storage, laundry, vending machines.

### Metcalf Hall

Floors: 3 + basement

Total Occupancy: 83

Bathrooms: Shared by wing

Coed: Yes

Residents: Mostly freshmen and sophomores; some juniors

Room Types: Singles, doubles, one sophomore triple

### (Metcalf Hall, continued)

Special Features: Bridge Program (organized faculty presentations to stimulate intellectual discussion), common room with TV and Ping-Pong, study lounges, second floor kitchen, bike storage, laundry, Scholar-in-Residence.

### Miller Hall

Floors: 4

Total Occupancy: 204

Bathrooms: Four single-sex bathrooms shared by floor

Coed: Yes, single-sex by room

Residents: Upperclassmen

Room Types: Doubles

Special Features: Oxfam Café, Ping-Pong, common room, study lounges, kitchen in dorm, bike storage, laundry, vending machines, surrounds courtyard (the Green).

### Richardson House

Floors: 3 + basement

Total Occupancy: 44

Bathrooms: Shared by floor

Coed: No (all female)

Residents: Freshmen and sophomores

Room Types: Singles, doubles

Special Features: Common room with TV, study lounges, ground floor kitchen, bike storage, laundry, vending machines, hardwood floors, former private residence, so all rooms are different.

### South Hall

Floors: 4

Total Occupancy: 378

Bathrooms: Shared by four to six students on floor

Coed: Yes, single-sex by room; second floor single-sex by wing

Residents: Freshmen and sophomores

Room Types: Singles, doubles

Special Features: Electronic card access, healthy living floor, elevator, common room with TV, study lounges, first floor kitchen, bike storage, laundry, points transfer machine, rooms have adjustable heat, located next to student parking lot.

### Stratton Hall

Floors: 3 + basement

Total Occupancy: 86

Bathrooms: Floors two and three share one bathroom; ground and first floor share two bathrooms

Coed: Yes, single-sex by floor

Residents: Upperclassmen

Room Types: Singles, doubles, one three-person apartment

Special Features: Study lounges, common rooms, laundry, hardwood floors, first floor kitchen, bike storage.

### Tilton Hall

Floors: 4 + basement

Total Occupancy: 150

Bathrooms: Shared by floor

Coed: Yes

## (Tilton Hall , continued)

Residents: Freshmen

Room Types: Doubles

Special Features: Common room with TV, study lounges, ground floor kitchen, bike storage, laundry, vending machines, Scholar-in-Residence.

## West Hall

Floors: 4 + basement

Total Occupancy: 95

Bathrooms: Shared by floor, some floors have more than one bathroom (first floor has no bathrooms)

Coed: Yes

Residents: Freshmen, sophomores

Room Types: Singles, doubles, triples (with common room), quads (with common room), one two-person apartment

Special Features: Common room with TV, study lounges, kitchen, bike storage, laundry, hardwood floors, vending machines, host of "December Naked Quad Run."

## Wilson House

Floors: 4

Total Occupancy: 55

Bathrooms: Shared by floor (third floor female bathroom only has one shower and one toilet)

Coed: Yes, single-sex by wing; ground floor is all male

Residents: Mostly upperclassmen

Room Types: Singles, doubles, and 5 triples

Special Features: Two common rooms (one with TV), first floor kitchen, Ping-Pong, laundry, basement mailboxes.

## Wren Hall

Floors: 4 + basement

Total Occupancy: 222

Bathrooms: Shared by suite

Coed: Yes, single-sex by suite (two showers, toilets, sinks)

Residents: Mostly upperclassmen

Room Types: 10-person suites (four doubles, two singles)

Special Features: Common room with TV and Ping-Pong, study lounges, common kitchen, bike storage, laundry, vending machines.

## Special-Interest Housing

In addition to the regular student housing, there are 15 special-interest housing units which offer undergrads the opportunity to live and further integrate with students who have interests similar to their own. Interested students must take the time to stop by the house they intend to live in and speak with students living there to demonstrate their interest. Students then apply for their particular house in the Office of Residential Life and Learning in South Hall.

Africana Unit
Capen House
8 Professors Row

The Arts House
Bartol House
37 Sawyer Avenue

Asian American Unit
Start House
17 Latin Way

Chinese House
A220-A229 Latin Way

The Crafts Unit
Anthony House
14 Professors Row

French Language Unit
Schmalz House
11 Whitfield Road

German Language Unit
Wyeth House
21 Whitfield Road

Latino Culture Unit
Milne House
8-10 Whitfield Road

International Culture Unit
Davies House
13 Sawyer Avenue

Japanese Language Unit
150s of Hillside Apts

Hall House
Jewish Culture Unit
98 Packard Ave.

Muslim Special Interest Unit
176 Curtis Street

Rainbow House
160s of Hillside Apts.

The Russian/Slavic Unit
101 Talbot Avenue

Spanish Language Unit
Chandler House
125 Powder House Boulevard

## Bed Type

Twin extra-long mattress (39" x 80"); some lofts, some bunk-beds

## Available for Rent

Minifridges

## Cleaning Services

Bathrooms and common rooms are cleaned by OneSource daily, except in on-campus apartments.

## You Get

Bed, dresser, desk, desk chair, closet or wardrobe, T-1 Ethernet connection (one per person), phone jack (one per room)

## Also Available

Cable television, special-interest houses, healthy-living options

## Did You Know?

Freshmen, as well as sophomores, are **required to live on campus** at Tufts.

Students recieve their requested **housing based on a lottery system**—which means that after freshman year, where you end up living may depend on how lucky you get with your lottery number that particular year.

### Students Speak Out On...
# Campus Housing

**"The dorms are decent. All uphill dorms are nice, except Wren Hall, and all the downhill dorms are bad, except for South Hall. Probably the best place to live as an underclassman is Miller Hall."**

"Dorms are, on the whole, pretty decent. Big dorms like South are fun and modern, but can also be isolating freshman year if you don't land on a good hall. People in Bush and Metcalf seem to have **good bonding experiences**. Stratton is good if you want big rooms and no noise. But it is so quiet sometimes, the place feels empty."

"No freshman has complained about all-freshman Tilton or Houston Hall, but I think that it is good to live and meet with sophomores when you first get to campus. Some of my best friends are in the year above or year below me because I lived in the same dorms as them. **Hanging out with all one class year limits you**. Bush hall, where I lived for two years, is a great dorm. No one usually knows much about it because it is pretty small. But it is right next to a dining hall and the Campus Center, and across the street from Tilton, so you can hang out with other freshmen. Also, Bush Hall is small enough that everyone on the floor usually becomes great friends."

"The dorms are all pretty good, but **Lewis, Carmichael, and Wren are boring for freshman**. Most of the people who live there are upperclassmen in singles, and they don't have the same community there."

Q "All the dorms are fine. **Miller is probably the best one for freshmen**, unless you want to live in the all-freshman dorm. I would try to avoid living in the O-zone (basement) of Wren or Haskell Hall, but you don't really have a choice."

Q "**I've seen better dorms**, but I've also seen dorms much worse than ours on other campuses. It's a conflict between uphill and downhill at Tufts: uphill has Miller and Houston, and the best downhill dorm is Bush. Tilton is the all-freshman dorm, which is great for making friends. Haskell and Wren are generally considered the bad dorms; they're the oldest and 'dirtiest,' but they're honestly not that bad. If you live in Hogdon or Carmichael, you can get food in the dining hall without leaving, so you never have to change out of your pajamas."

Q "The dorms are pretty nice. **Wren and Haskell are suite-style**—four doubles and two singles to a group. The other dorms are just big buildings with tons of rooms. For freshman year, I liked having the bigger dorm to get to know people, but I guess later on the other two would be nice."

Q "The dorms are pretty good; friends at other universities who have visited say that Tufts' dorms are beautiful. **Miller is best for freshmen**, West is best for sophomores, and Wren and Haskell are the worst."

Q "You're assigned a room freshman year, so you don't have any choice. Most of the dorms are pretty nice, but the newer ones with nicer facilities have smaller rooms. Older ones with larger rooms have **shadier bathrooms and other questionable facilities**. Tufts is loosely split into two areas, creatively titled 'uphill' and 'downhill.' Uphill dorms are generally a little bigger, but the uphill dining hall, Carmichael, is not as good."

Q "Tufts is on a hill, and **all of the academic buildings are uphill**. If you live uphill, you are close to all your classes. If you live downhill, you are five to ten minutes closer to the subway station, and closer to the student center and lots of other recreational places. There is a dining hall uphill, and a dining hall downhill, yet the better one is downhill."

Q "The dorms are all nice in some way. Some are **nice in appearance, but have smaller rooms**; some aren't as nice looking, and have big rooms. In some, you live in a suite with other people. Your best pick depends on what you are looking for. There is also the all-female dorm and the all-freshman dorm. If you don't want to live with guys, I heard that the all-female is pretty nice. I wouldn't recommend the all-freshman dorm—it seems like those kids take more time to mature because they don't have the older kids around them to ask for advice."

Q "Dorms are pretty nice, in general, but Miller and Houston Halls are considered the best freshman dorms. **Housing's done completely by lottery**, so you won't know where you will be housed until the beginning of August. Dorms to avoid, although you don't have much control over it your first year, are Haskell and Wren."

Q "As a freshman, they place you into a random dorm with a random roommate. I say 'random roommate,' but **it's not quite random**—you fill out a survey describing your interests, and Tufts does its best to match you up."

# The College Prowler Take On...
# Campus Housing

Tufts dorm rooms aren't the size of hotel lobbies, but they aren't the size of hotel closets, either. Some dorms are slightly better than others, but most rooms are medium-sized, and living in any one of them is a similar experience. Students will exhibit a preference for newer or recently renovated dorms like South and Miller. West, Stratton, and Metcalf have an old, historic building style; they also have larger rooms. Most students will say that the worst dorms are Haskell and Wren, which were built in the '70s and haven't really been renovated since. The fact remains, however, that no matter what dorm you're assigned during your first year, the differences are going to be small.

For junior and senior year, there are more options, but also more of a chance that you will live off campus—housing is only guaranteed for freshman and sophomore year. There is, however, a definite distinction between uphill and downhill dorms in terms of convenience. Once you live in one location, you can never really move to the other without changing your view of Tufts. Overall, housing isn't too much of a concern during your first year because you don't really have any control over where you stay. The silver lining is that none of your classmates will either. Furthermore, you'll all get at least two semesters to check out what areas you like the best before you choose your housing for the years to come.

**B-**

The College Prowler® Grade on

Campus
Housing: B-

A high Campus Housing grade indicates that dorms are clean, well-maintained and spacious. Other determining factors include variety of dorms, proximity to classes and social atmosphere.

# Off-Campus Housing

The Lowdown On...
## Off-Campus Housing

**Undergrads in Off-Campus Housing:**
25%

**Average Rent for:**
**1-BR Apt.:** $900–$1,000
**2-BR Apt.:** $1,200–$1,800
**3-BR Apt.:** $1,800–$2,100
**4-BR Apt.:** $2,100–$3,000

**Best Time to Look For a Place:**
First semester of sophomore year

**Popular Areas:**
Boston Avenue, Bromfield Road, Chetwynd Road, College Avenue, Pearson Road, Powderhouse Boulevard, Sunset Avenue

## For Assistance Contact

Off-Campus Housing Resource Center

South Hall, Lower Campus Road

(617) 627-5319

*http://ase.tufts.edu/och*

E-Mail: och@tufts.edu

Hours: Monday–Friday 9 a.m.–3 p.m.

## Students Speak Out On...
# Off-Campus Housing

"Many times, getting housing junior year is in a class all by itself. Be sure to start early to find the best rentals so you can live with your friends."

Q "Living off campus is really nice, and gives you **much more space and independence compared to the dorms**. Finding housing off campus is not as hard as people say, but you have to know where to look, and what to look for."

Q "Living off campus is amazing. I moved off campus after sophomore year, and **I never want to move back on campus**. The off-campus houses are very close to campus. They are student houses, but they are nicer (and much bigger) than on-campus rooms and apartments. Living off campus is more expensive, but it's definitely worth it."

Q "Juniors are hard-pressed to find campus housing, but off-campus abodes are **close, affordable, and generally pretty nice**. I haven't met anyone who has had a bad experience with their residence."

Q "Unfortunately, housing **off campus is often necessary after sophomore year**. Sophomores have among the worst lottery numbers, but are still guaranteed housing. Therefore, they often get the smallest rooms available. As for the junior class, they are always dealing with the threat of being homeless for the duration of junior year. There is no longer guaranteed housing after sophomore year, and the landlords around campus have come to realize it."

Q "A student will end up paying an **exorbitant amount of money in rent** to stay on campus if they do not start looking for an off-campus house around the beginning of sophomore year."

Q "For me, it would not be convenient because it's very expensive. I think **it's better to live on campus**, but it goes in cycles. My junior year, everybody went off campus, and did so with ease. This year, there was a huge crunch. There are many funky little houses nearby that the University rents out. If you get organized with housemates early and go looking, it's no problem."

Q "There are lots of fun apartments on campus and many **more options off campus**. I lived on campus for two years, and now I live off campus. Most people do the same, moving off campus junior year."

Q "Housing off campus is convenient, and there is a lot of it. Most people live in houses and apartments off campus when they are juniors and seniors. There are a lot of places in the area surrounding the school, and the **prices aren't outrageous**. Freshman and sophomore year, you are guaranteed housing, and must live in on-campus housing unless you commute or are under special circumstances."

Q "Off-campus housing is probably the single biggest complaint of the junior class. **They're not guaranteed housing**, and most people, depending on the lottery numbers that determine housing preferences, may have to go find a place to live off campus where the rent is pretty high. Some people prefer to live off campus because they like the freedom, but on-campus housing is substantially cheaper, and it's nice that you don't have to clean. It's not hard to get a place to live around campus, because most of the area surrounding Tufts is residential, but it's tough to find the right house at the right price unless you get started early."

Q "We are in a residential area, and almost all houses surrounding campus rent to Tufts students. We found our off-campus house that we lived in for the last two years without a problem. Rent is high at about $600 per month, but **it's not that much higher than dorm living**."

Q "I know people who have enjoyed living in the dorms all four years. If you stay on campus, you can get apartment-style housing instead of the dorms, too. The off-campus apartments can be quite affordable—I'm a **10 minute walk from campus** in a 4-bedroom apartment with a huge kitchen, and I only pay $500 a month."

### The College Prowler Take On...
# Off-Campus Housing

Moving off campus is both a blessing and a curse for most Tufts students. Every year, about 40 percent of the junior class goes abroad, in part to experience a different culture, and in part to avoid searching for an off-campus apartment. As Davis Square becomes increasingly popular, rent prices near Tufts have almost no ceiling and are continually on the rise. Seniors are expressing a bigger desire to move back onto campus for their last year, and this forces juniors to move off campus.

Renting can be difficult—utility bills become a worry, you have to consider the safety of the place you're living, and deal with often antagonistic landlords. However, many students enjoy the independence of having their own places, and living with friends can add to the comfort level and social dimension of the Tufts experience. Chances are you'll make friends with at least a few upperclassmen who live on their own, and this can give you a better idea of what to look for when you're deciding on housing for your later years. If you do choose to go for a house or apartment, it's important to find roommates early and start looking as quickly as you can—September and October aren't too soon to consider signing a lease for the coming summer.

B-

**The College Prowler® Grade on**

Off-Campus
Housing: B-

A high grade in Off-Campus Housing indicates that apartments are of high quality, close to campus, affordable, and easy to secure.

# Diversity

The Lowdown On...
## Diversity

**African American:**
5%

**Native American:**
Less than 1%

**Asian American:**
13%

**White:**
55%

**Hispanic:**
5%

**Unknown:**
11%

**International:**
10%

**Out-of-State:**
78%

# Political Activity

Tufts is a very politically-charged campus. Though most students would probably consider themselves centrist or leaning to the left, the front pages of the campus newspaper are often covered with loud, public battles between a sect of radical liberals and a sect of reactionary conservatives.

# Gay Pride

In past years, there were a few hate crimes each semester on campus, but those numbers have been dwindling in recent years. Except for a few isolated incidents every once in a while, the campus is very tolerant, and most students are very supportive of the gay community. This community is very active—celebrating everything from Coming Out Day to Gay Pride Month. There is also a special living unit called the Rainbow House, where coed rooming is allowed. Every year, Tufts sponsors the Safe Colleges Conference for student movements all over the country, complete with a drag show.

# Minority Clubs

There are so many minority, cultural, and ethnic clubs on campus that they have their own Cultural Coordinating Committee (CCC) to coordinate activities. There is some debate in the student government whether these groups deserve special representation or not. The Caribbean Club, a **South Asian literary magazine**, and the Association of Latin American Students (ALAS) are very active on campus. The groups work in recruiting minority students to campus, mentoring programs in the community, and promotions of all different kinds of cultural activities on campus.

# Economic Status

Tufts students come from all economic levels, but since Tufts' endowment is somewhat miniscule for its tier, there are many students who are not receiving any financial aid. Thus, there is a huge population of very wealthy kids, many of them international students. There is also a huge population of students receiving financial aid. Students don't really discuss their differing economic status; they focus more on academics, though, many students say that they are simply surprised by the amount of money some of their classmates can have.

# Most Popular Religions

There are a number of active religious communities on campus. Students are involved in a few different Christian organizations, and there is a large and active Jewish community. The Islamic community on campus is growing, and there are also a number of Eastern religions represented on campus (Hindi, Buddhist, and Bahai).

## Students Speak Out On...
# Diversity

> **"I think the campus is pretty diverse. Despite that, however, it seems that most people hang out with people of similar culture or nationality. There are cliques that are, to a certain extent, based on race."**

Q "**People complain a lot that the campus really isn't that diverse**, but I think that while it is diverse, the different ethnic and racial groups tend to factionalize themselves a bit. I think a lot of people do it, and it's understandable to a degree because you hang out with the people with whom you identify, but I think it tends to be divisive when it becomes exclusive."

Q "I think the campus is extremely diverse, culturally and ethnically, though, perhaps **not as much economically**."

Q "**Tufts is very diverse**. This is my favorite part about Tufts."

Q "The campus is fairly diverse, though, the administration does not seem to value diversity as much as it claims. We have had **a number of hate crimes on campus** in the last few years, and there has not been enough done in my opinion to counteract them. There is an active lesbian/gay and bisexual/transvestite group, and Tufts is a fairly friendly place for an alternative lifestyle."

Q "**Tufts is progressively becoming more diverse**. There are many clubs for different ethnic and cultural groups. I know the Latino population has grown, and I think the same goes for many of the minority groups. I would argue that diversity is the great strength of Tufts."

Q "We have a very diverse student body—it's something admissions is very aggressive about. There are **lots of international students**, and students of different ethnic and religious backgrounds. There are all sorts of culture clubs that provide a positive environment. As a white, upper-class, Anglo-Saxon, Protestant male, I think that the diversity of Tufts taught me more than anything else."

Q "Campus is diverse, but like most colleges, **the disparate groups often don't interact well**. I don't feel bad in saying it since this is a problem common to almost every college, but I think the barrier can be broken if you do want to hang out with different people. I do, and I happen to like it."

Q "Tufts is known for its **high percentage of international students**. I have friends from India, Switzerland, England, France, Costa Rica, Colombia, and Persia."

### The College Prowler Take On...
# Diversity

On matriculation day, students may see a lot of different looking faces, but they may never have actually interacted with them during the year. This is one of the most unfortunate situations at Tufts, and increasing the admissions numbers is only going to help so much. As happens at many schools, students at Tufts tend to hang out with others in their own ethnic/social groups, so there is a notable amount of self-segregation. These groups get along quite well, but by and large, don't have much interaction.

Despite the social scene, however, Tufts does have students from every walk of life. Well over a quarter of the student body is composed of minorities, and cultural groups on campus are very active. These groups are many, and range from the Pan-African Alliance, the Asian American Club, the South Asian Club, the Association of Latin American Students, and the Caribbean Club. Tufts students hail from all over America and all over the world. If you're open to meeting new people and learning from them, there are plenty of opportunities for a diverse and unique experience at Tufts.

**B+**

The College Prowler® Grade on
Diversity: B+

A high grade in Diversity indicates that ethnic minorities and international students have a notable presence on campus, and that students of different economic backgrounds, religious beliefs, and sexual preferences are well-represented.

# Guys & Girls

### The Lowdown On...
## Guys & Girls

**Female Undergrads:**
51%

**Male Undergrads:**
49%

### Birth Control Available?
Yes, from Health Services

### Best Place to Meet Guys/Girls
In the dorms, at frat parties, off-campus parties, and in the Wilderness Group

## Social Scene

While other prestigious schools nearby might be buried in their books, Tufts students, while still studious, won't hesitate to leave their books behind and all of a sudden turn into "people people." There are parties going on every weekend, in every corner of campus (or off-campus for that matter), and often, students will take their parties into Boston or Davis Square. There is a certain amount of camaraderie among all students in the Boston area, and they are pretty willing to have any Tufts student come to parties. Though cliques may develop around certain extracurricular activities, no group is exclusive, and they are always looking for new people to tag along. Since first-year students are all on the same meal plan and don't have much homework yet, they tend to spend a lot of time hanging out in dining halls and common rooms. Sophomores, juniors, and seniors pretty much have their friends from their year, and parties become more exciting and common with the passing of each year.

## Hookups or Relationships?

Freshman year is dominated by "freshman lust," and freshman relations mainly consist of hookups, except for those few couples who meet the first week of school and stay together until finals week of senior year when they finally realize that they aren't right for each other. Halfway through sophomore year, people begin to pair off and generally stay paired off through junior and senior year. A lot of students complain that by their third year, all the guys or girls worth being with at Tufts are taken. Fortunately for those still unattached, Boston is ripe with students from 55 other colleges.

## Dress Code

Tufts students either have their own really unique style, or that standard New England college fare—collared shirts and jeans for the guys; tank tops, jeans, black pants, and tall black shoes for the girls.

## Did You Know?

**Top Three Places to Find Hotties:**

1. Frat parties
2. Dance extracurriculars (i.e., Tufts Dance Collective, Spirit of Color)
3. Drama classes

**Top Five Places to Hook Up:**

1. The Tisch Library roof
2. Behind a frat house
3. Your freshman dorm room
4. The Memorial steps
5. Common rooms

Students Speak Out On...
# Guys & Girls

{ **"Smart people are not, on average, good-looking. That goes for guys and girls. Both fall into the J.Crew stereotype pretty well a lot of the time, but not always."**

Q "**Lots of people just hook up with other people**, and then you have your die-hard couples who are joined at the hip and rarely go anywhere unaccompanied by their other half, but I think there are plenty of people who don't do either, be it because they are dating someone at another school, or just not really dating anyone."

Q "**The guys are dorky, but cute**. But there are lots of different types of guys out there. There are some hot guys, but they're not everywhere."

Q "There are definitely standards of guys or girls which are more prevalent at Tufts, but on the whole, it's a very diverse place, and guys or girls are different enough from one another to prevent general stereotyping. The people seem **generally friendly, interesting, and open-minded**."

Q "The girls at Tufts are definitely better looking than the guys. Although it's true that **people don't really fix themselves up at Tufts** as much as at schools, say, in the South. Girls in general dress more casual, except for the international folks, who are always dressed to the nines."

Q "I think **everyone is pretty nice** as far as appearance goes. Tufts definitely has a lack of hot guys. Most of them are pretty smart and nice, but not as attractive as one might hope."

**Q** "I get really sick of this scene because it can seem like a bunch of rich kids at a good school who are here so they can be rich adults in the future. There's **too much focus on material things**, and too many spoiled kids who don't comprehend the value of their education because they haven't had to struggle to get here. There's also a lot of apathy about what is wrong in the world. There are many things I'm frustrated with here, but from what I hear, these problems exist at every elite private school."

**Q** "Guys have the reputation for being **short, Jewish, and dorky**. There are exceptions to this, obviously, and all you really need is one or two guys to focus on. The guys at Tufts aren't the best part, but you can find your match, and the other benefits outweigh this seemingly negative aspect. The girls here are awesome—I didn't have many close female friends in high school, but at Tufts, all my friends are girls."

**Q** "There are a lot of nerds here, but there are definitely a lot of people who are down to party, too. The people at Tufts aren't really good-looking, but there are **so many college kids in Boston** that it's not a problem."

**Q** "Tufts is small enough to **feel super comfortable**, see familiar faces, and know people wherever you go, but there are still a gazillion people to meet that you have never seen before."

**Q** "It's **a very well-dressed campus**—not snobby or ridiculously dressy, but people make an effort to look nice."

**Q** "This school is **notorious for having ugly girls**. It's a campus-wide running joke that Tufts has the most hurt girls. If you're an attractive woman, you will have your choice of guys. The guys, mostly from the Midwest and East Coast, are pretty snobbish, arrogant, and stuck up. These words come to mind: Abercrombie & Fitch, lacrosse, and import beer."

Q "Tufts is said to not be a very attractive campus, but I don't think it's that bad. There are some really good-looking guys, and many very sweet ones. One of my friends told me I should go to Tufts since the girls weren't all that attractive, and I would have an easy time finding guys. This wasn't altogether true, but **it does help to not go to school with a lot of supermodels**."

Q "There's the full range of geeks to jocks, granola tree-huggers to **Banana Republic princesses**. Guys complain that there aren't any hot girls, but these are also probably the same guys who aren't getting any dates, so it's hard to tell."

Q "There's a weird reputation that Tufts has ugly people, but I disagree with that. **Tufts has 4,500 people**—you are bound to find someone you like!"

Q "**I haven't really had a problem finding cute boys**. I feel like if you're pretty and reasonably different, you won't have a problem finding a beau. The girls are pretty, so I see the girls as being hotter on the whole than the guys."

Q "You have your mix of stuck-up rich girls and really nice, down-to-earth ones. **It takes time to find your crowd**, but you will eventually. The guys are well mixed, too. They aren't California-surfer dudes by any means, but they are, overall, pretty good-looking. Finding an all-round great guy can be a challenge, unless you're really lucky."

Q "**People from Tufts are cool**. They're not the best-looking people, but keep in mind, they are smart."

### The College Prowler Take On...
# Guys & Girls

You can generalize Tufts guys and girls, and still be fairly accurate. They aren't the best looking—usually a bit on the dorky side—and probably weren't super-popular in high school, but still really enjoy partying and socializing. Although Tufts is not a huge school, there are enough students (and a relatively even mix of guys and girls) that you're sure to find attractive coeds. Many students agree that the athletes are particularly hot, especially the soccer and lacrosse players.

As far as the dating scene goes, freshmen are generally single; about halfway through sophomore year, people begin pairing off. If you're still a loner by senior year, you'll probably find yourself surrounded by couples. Once everyone is attached, it seems like the dating scene is nonexistent and that all the good ones are taken. Never fear—Boston has thousands upon thousands of college students passing through every year, so there is always hope and plenty of opportunities to meet new people.

**The College Prowler® Grade on**
## Guys: C

A high grade for Guys indicates that the male population on campus is attractive, smart, friendly, and engaging, and that the school has a decent ratio of guys to girls.

**The College Prowler® Grade on**
## Girls: C+

A high grade for Girls not only implies that the women on campus are attractive, smart, friendly, and engaging, but also that there is a fair ratio of girls to guys.

# Athletics

The Lowdown On...
## Athletics

**Athletic Division:**
Division III

**Conference:**
New England Small College
(NESCAC)

**School Mascot:**
Jumbo (PT Barnum's
cherished elephant)

**Men Playing
Varsity Sports:**
402 (18%)

**Women Playing
Varsity Sports:**
356 (14%)

→

## Men's Varsity Sports:

Baseball

Basketball

Crew

Cross-Country

Football

Golf

Ice Hockey

Lacrosse

Sailing

Soccer

Squash

Swimming & Diving

Tennis

Track & Field

## Club Sports:

Cycling (Coed)

Equestrian (Coed)

Fencing (Men's)

Rugby (Men's and Women's)

Skiing (Coed)

Table Tennis

Ultimate Frisbee (Men's and Women's)

Ultimate Frisbee (Women's)

Volleyball (Men's)

Water Polo (Coed)

## Women's Varsity Sports:

Basketball

Crew

Cross-Country

Fencing

Field Hockey

Golf

Lacrosse

Lightweight Crew

Sailing

Soccer

Softball

Squash

Swimming & Diving

Tennis

Track & Field

Volleyball

## Intramurals:

Badminton

Basketball

Dodgeball

Flag Football

Futsal (Indoor Soccer)

Softball

Tennis

Volleyball

Whiffleball

## Athletic Fields
Alumni Field, Ellis Oval, Fletcher Field

## Most Popular Sports
Men's basketball, women's basketball, men's football, men's baseball, women's soccer, men's soccer, sailing

## Overlooked Teams
Crew, ultimate Frisbee, women's volleyball

## Best Place to Take a Walk
Down Powderhouse Boulevard, past the rotary, and through to the little community park

# Gyms/Facilities

### Ames Human Performance Center
Ames is a physical performance center located in Cousens Gym for Tuft's athletes, as well as other students. The facility was recently updated with new equipment, including two circuits of Cybex machines, many aerobic machines, strength equipment, and free-weights. The facility also has a full-time strength and conditioning specialist as well as a sports medicine staff.

### Cousens Gym
Cousens is the largest gym on campus. The Cage has practice basketball and volleyball courts, and a batting cage. There are a number of other basketball courts throughout the building. Hamilton Pool, a sauna, squash courts, and the Lunder Fitness Center (with weights and exercise machines) are also located here. The Fitness Center gets crowded at night, and in January and February after everyone has made New Year's resolutions. The best time to go is in the morning.

## Gantcher Center

The Gantcher Center is brand new and state-of-the art. It has six indoor tennis courts, and an indoor track that the winners of the Boston Marathon trained on. It is often used for really big events like the First Freshman Class Dinner, and speeches by prominent people like Bill Clinton and George H.W. Bush.

## Jackson Gym

The smallest gym on campus, it is mainly home to a few gym classes, but also dance practices and career fairs.

## Tennis Courts

Outdoor tennis courts are sprinkled throughout the campus. You can use them whenever the tennis team is not using them. Though there are fewer South Hall Courts, generally, there is less of a line than at the Packard Avenue Courts.

## Students Speak Out On...
# Athletics

> **"Tufts is not big on its sports. People definitely play and enjoy going to games, but it is not a campus spirit builder."**

Q "Sports? Tufts has sports teams? Oh! That's what they were doing on that field! No, seriously, the best sports at Tufts are the club sports, like skiing and ultimate Frisbee. They mesh well with the college lifestyle and are a lot of fun—competitive, without cramping your style. If you are big into varsity athletics, just **be prepared to not have too many fans at the games**."

Q "Tufts is only a D-III school, and nobody really watches the sports. There are people who go to games, but they're not really Tufts students. There are a lot of older people coming to watch the games, and they just make parking worse on campus. **School spirit has nothing to do with sports**."

Q "**Most sports here are Division III**. Most Tufts teams are not very good. But if you choose to do a sport, it's a big time commitment. Intramural sports are a fun way to do a sport without the big commitment. IM sports aren't huge, but they are easy to find if you are looking for them."

Q "Sports at Tufts aren't the hottest thing ever, but I love going to Jumbo's games. We're not a D-I school, so **it isn't particularly action-packed or exciting**, but I love going to games. In the fall, football games are especially awesome."

Q "A lot of people are on teams, but they don't really have followings. **Our football team sucks**, but Tufts sailing is the best sailing team ever. We've won more championships in our sailing history than any other school. We have a bunch of club sports that compete close to varsity level. Intramurals are really just a bunch of friends who are on a team."

Q "Lots of people are involved in sports, but since it's a Division III school, **the varsity games aren't anything like you see on TV**. There are still a lot of people involved in the sports, and a lot of intramural sports on campus. It's just tough figuring out when and where they are."

Q "Other than Homecoming and the Naked Quad Run (which is what it sounds like), **there really isn't much school spirit** at Tufts. I wish there was more of it because the people are really great, and the athletes are very talented. IM sports are pretty big, but you have to be organized about it, or things just slip."

Q "Varsity sports, depending on which, are big on campus. I think **the biggest ones are track, soccer, softball, crew, and sailing**. Those teams have recently won championships at a national level, and are really popular. I was going to play varsity lacrosse, but it's a lot of work to be juggling hard courses, two jobs, and a social life."

Q "The teams are competitive, but school spirit is low. It's one of Tufts's biggest flaws. **The IM teams are pretty popular**, though, since most people do not want to commit to varsity or could not make the team or get enough playing time."

## The College Prowler Take On...
# Athletics

The University certainly doesn't own any kind of athletic bragging rights over any other schools, which is why those who believe sports are the essence of college have probably never heard of Tufts. A little known fact, though, is that the first American college football game took place between Tufts and Harvard. Tufts has a long-standing tradition of athletics, but most students find that school spirit is not focused around sports at all.

Tufts does have a couple of pretty good teams, and the competition in the NESCAC keeps things interesting. When a team is doing well, Tufts students will support it. Intramurals and club sports are popular, and the gym is always crowded—it's not that Tufts students are not athletic—they are just content to enjoy sports for the fun of the game, and are not looking for all the fanfare you might find at some larger state schools.

**The College Prowler® Grade on**

**Athletics: C-**

A high grade in Athletics indicates that students have school spirit, that sports programs are respected, that games are well-attended, and that intramurals are a prominent part of student life.

# Nightlife

**The Lowdown On...**
## Nightlife

## Club Prowler:
### Popular Nightlife Spots!

### Club Crawler:

#### Avalon
15 Lansdowne St., Boston
(617) 262-2424
*www.avalonboston.com*
Avalon is a spacious dance club and a live music venue. Go to see the band or party until it closes. You must be 19 or older to get into the dance club.

#### Axis
13 Lansdowne St., Boston
(617) 262-2437
*www.avalonboston.com*
Axis has two levels, so it's twice the fun, and you're bound to meet college students from all over Boston here. You must be 19 to enter during the week.

#### Bill's Bar
5 1/2 Lansdowne St., Boston
(617) 421-9678
Great live bands, moderate drink prices, and plenty of action.

➔

### Embassy

13 Lansdowne St., Boston

(617) 536-2100

Check out this dance club—a favorite among Tufts students. There is a more upscale dress code, and again, you must be at least 19 to enter.

### Jillian's

145 Ipswich St., Boston

(617) 437-0300

*www.jilliansboston.com*

Jillian's is enormous with a bar, dance club, pool tables, and even bowling. You must be at least 18 years old to get in, but after 8 p.m., the bar is 21 and older.

### Johnny D's Uptown

17 Holland St., Davis Square, Somerville

(617) 776-2004

*http://johnnydsuptown.com*

A live music club close to campus, Johnny D's also has a restaurant serving up an awesome brunch on Sundays.

### Jake Ivory's

9 Lansdowne St., Boston

(617) 247-1222

*www.jakeivorys.com*

This is a lively dueling piano bar that tends to be a bit expensive. You must be 21 and up on Fridays and Saturdays.

### The Roxy

279 Tremont St., Boston

(617) 338-7699

*www.roxyboston.com*

A cozier kind of feel in the middle of the Theater District, Roxy is a unique kind of club and has lots of specialty nights. There are 18-and-over nights, as well.

## Bar Prowler:

### The Burren

247 Elm St., Davis Square, Somerville

(617) 776-6896

*www.burren.com*

Genuine traditional Irish bar with Irish music. Check out the Thursday night house band, a favorite of Tufts students. Must be 21 to enter.

### Cheers Bull & Finch

Pub 84 Beacon St., Boston

(617) 227-9605

*www.cheersboston.com*

Everyone might not know your name here, but this is the real Cheers which inspired the classic TV show. You won't find Sam Malone around, but still, it's a happening bar with good burgers.

### Christopher's

1920 Massachusetts Ave., Cambridge

(617) 876-9180

A bar with its own character, a good place to chill with friends, and not too far from Tufts in Porter Square.

### Hong Kong Restaurant

1238 Massachusetts Ave., Cambridge

(617) 864-5311

The scorpion bowl drinks are worth the trip, but the Chinese food is nothing special. This is also a comedy club during the week and a dance club on the weekends.

### John Harvard's Brew House

33 Dunster St., Cambridge

(617) 868-3585

*www.johnharvards.com*

Try their great original brews and their food, as well. Monday nights have half-price appetizers for students after 10 p.m.

### The Joshua Tree Bar & Grill

256 Elm St., Somerville

(617) 623-9910

*www.joshuatreebarand grill.com*

It's loud in here, but that's just because of the crowds. Come for the beer on tap and the great food. Try the salads, but get there early so you can hear when people talk to you.

### Redbones/Underbones

55 Chester St., Davis Square, Somerville

(617) 628-2200

*www.redbonesbbq.com*

This is a popular bar for Tufts students. Try all their grilled specialties. The basement of Redbones is called Underbones. It's also worth noting that this bar does not accept credit cards—just good ole'-fashioned cash.

### TT the Bear's Place

10 Brookline St., Cambridge

(617) 492-2327

*www.ttthebears.com*

A legendary live music venue, TT's shouldn't be missed.

**Bars Close At:**

2 a.m.

**Primary Areas with Nightlife:**

Davis Square
Harvard Square
Lansdowne Street

**Cheapest Place to Get a Drink:**

Underbones

**Favorite Drinking Games:**

Beer Pong
Card Games
Century Club
Kings
Power Hour
Quarters

**Student Favorites:**

Avalon
Axis
The Burren
RedBones/Underbones

## What to Do if You're Not 21

There are plenty of cool things for under-agers to do around Boston. Most clubs' age requirement is 19 just to dance, and the Diesel Café, located at 257 Elm Street in Davis Square, has some nice pool tables and makes a killer latte. The Café is open until 1 a.m. on the weekends, and 12 a.m. during the week (*www.diesel-cafe.com*). The Somerville Theater (*www.somervilletheatreonline.com*), a historic landmark in Boston, can be found at 55 Davis Square. It's a great place to check out for live music and movies, and the facility has an awesome old-fashioned feel. Lastly, no one should miss the Rocky Horror Picture Show put on in Harvard Square.

## Useful Resources for Nightlife

*www.bostonphoenix.com*
*www.clubvibes.com*
*www.bostonnightguide.com*

## Students Speak Out On...
# Nightlife

**"The clubbing scene is available to those who are interested in it. Lansdowne Street has a ton of clubs for 19-and-older, but these can get expensive fairly quickly if you go a lot."**

Q "The bars are decent, but **they are strict about underage drinking**. The clubs in Boston are fun, but they are 19-and-over, so most freshmen can't go. The only problem with going to clubs in Boston is that you'll have to take a cab back to campus, but it's worth it."

Q "**Parties on campus have kegger written all over them**, and they can be kind of sad sometimes. The frat scene is great for freshmen; it allows them to go out and get blasted, and run into people from all over campus, but the scene gets tired (or rather, should) by sophomore year. Dorm parties and house parties come into play then, and sometimes it requires a little work to find. It's getting tougher to hold off-campus parties because the local police shut them down often because of neighbors' complaints, and the frats are in a lot of trouble these days because of a number of issues in the past few years, so that might die this year, too. Students have more and more incentives to go into Boston."

Q "Around Tufts, **there are a bunch of very townie local bars**, but they are fun Thursdays—the big college night—and they're very lenient about carding. There are also many clubs and bars at Lansdowne Street and Fanueil Hall. The bar scene is much better than the clubs, but the clubs are nice, too, I suppose."

Q "For bars and clubs, we usually go into Boston where you have a million places to go. One of my favorite clubs is Avalon, which on weekends, is connected to two other clubs—so when you are in, you can go from club to club without a problem. Each club had **its own music style**. As you can imagine, in such a big city there are a ton of bars. When you don't feel like going into the city, you can always enjoy a night at the frats, which I have to say is very fun."

Q "Unfortunately, **everything shuts down early in Boston**. By 2 a.m. all the clubs close, which kind of sucks. It really depends on what kind of music you like. Avalon is good for techno, and Embassy for Latin. I have always been disappointed when I have gone out to a club. My best bet is always a party held by one of the universities—they seem to have the best music."

Q "The Somerville Theater gets a lot of musical groups, Johnny D's has live jazz most nights and a DJ a couple nights a week, and the Burren has live Irish music and a cover band that plays good rock. The big dance clubs are mostly on **Lansdowne Street in Boston**, which is a short T-ride away. If you feel like getting all dressed up, the best choice is Avalon, which is 19-plus on Thursday and Friday nights. It's rated among the five best nightclubs in the world!"

Q "All the clubs in Boston are **expensive and hard to get into**. A drawback of Boston is that everything pretty much closes at 2 a.m., including the train, called the T, which stops running a little after 12 a.m."

# The College Prowler Take On...
# Nightlife

As far as local options go, there are a lot of very nice bars close to Tufts—particularly in Davis Square. If you really want to dance, though, you'll probably have to head down to Lansdowne Street in Boston. The bars and clubs there, in the broadest sense, are exclusive, but expensive. Given the huge number of organization parties, house parties, and fraternity events right around the University, Tufts students don't have to leave the campus area to have a good time. Besides, it's more convenient, and ultimately more affordable, for students to remain on campus grounds and attend a frat party (five dollars to drink all night, usually free for girls).

Boston has a huge college population to support, so there is always avid nightlife to be found in the city. Tufts students have the benefit of quantity and variety in regards to bars, clubs, and parties, and students won't be left longing for wild times as long as they're willing to meet new people and get out and look for new places. So, the two biggest downsides here are that many clubs are overly-expensive, and everything in the city closes at 2 a.m. Tufts also has its own scene of parties and shows, but many students like to venture off campus looking for a little added spice over the weekends.

The College Prowler® Grade on

Nightlife: A-

A high grade in Nightlife indicates that there are many bars and clubs in the area that are easily accessible and affordable. Other determining factors include the number of options for the under-21 crowd and the prevalence of house parties.

# Greek Life

The Lowdown On...
## Greek Life

**Number of Fraternities:**
10

**Undergrad Men in Fraternities:**
15%

**Number of Sororities:**
3

**Undergrad Women in Sororities:**
4%

## Fraternities on Campus:

Alpha Epsilon Pi

Alpha Tau Omega

Delta Tau Delta

Delta Upsilon

Sigma Nu

Sigma Phi Epsilon

Theta Chi

Theta Delta Chi

Zeta Beta Tau

Zeta Psi

## Sororities on Campus:

Alpha Omicron Pi

Alpha Phi

Chi Omega

## Other Greek Organizations:

Bi-Cultural Inter-Greek Council

Interfraternity Council

Inter-Greek Council (IGC)

Panhellenic Council

Order of Omega

## Multicultural Colonies:

Alpha Kappa Alpha Sorority

Alpha Phi Alpha Fraternity

Alpha Rho Lambda Sorority

Delta Sigma Theta Sorority

Kappa Alpha Psi Fraternity

Lambda Upsilon Lambda (La Unidad Latina) Fraternity

Omega Phi Beta Sorority

Omega Psi Phi Fraternity

Phi Beta Sigma Fraternity

Sigma Lambda Upsilon (Señoritas Latinas Unidas) Sorority

Zeta Phi Beta Sorority

## Students Speak Out On...
# Greek Life

**"There are so many more frats than sororities, and you don't have to be a part of the Greek system at this school, unlike other schools."**

Q "Tufts is **not much of a party school**. There are a few frats, and they have parties occasionally. There is usually something going on every weekend, but some weekends, you'll have to look hard to find a party. On the big weekends, the parties are good. DTD and ZBT have the best parties."

Q "Greek life dominates much of the underclassman social scene, but that's because they have many beginning-of-the-year parties for people to get to know each other. Not many people are actually in the houses, but **many people go to their parties**."

Q "**Parties revolve around the frats** for maybe your first two years. This scene is a lot of fun at first, but can get old fairly quickly. House parties are typically smaller, but upperclassmen tend to invite just friends, so these can be more close-knit and a good time."

Q "There is Greek life here, but it definitely does not dominate the social scene. The frats are a fun place to go on the weekends, but **they tend to be pretty quiet when they are not having a party**. There are three sororities, but they aren't allowed to have parties, so frats basically make up all of the Greek life."

Q "The Greek life is very good. I enjoy going to the frat parties, especially to meet people. I'm in a sorority, and I think joining was **one of the best choices I made** my freshman year at Tufts. The Greek life kind of dominates the social scene, but there are also other clubs that constantly give parties, such as the dance teams, that you can go to if the Greek system is not your thing."

Q "Greek life is pretty prominent—lots of people like to go party at the frats on weekends. Most of the time **their parties are free to get into**, and they give away free beer. Sometimes, though, they get really crowded and are hard to get into, so you just have to be patient."

Q "Greek life **plays a big role in the social scene**, especially when there's nothing huge elsewhere on campus, but most people who go choose willingly to do so. I prefer house parties to frats, but they're definitely available for those who want them. Greeks play a big role in the social scene, but it really depends on what kind of good time you're looking for."

Q "I am in a sorority, but there are only three—they definitely do not dominate campus. A lot of people who go out to party are in the Greek system—mostly the boys. Most of the sports teams have houses on campus, but **frats aren't everything at Tufts**. There are always house parties, and Boston rocks."

Q "Greek life isn't dominant at all. The frats have parties, though the sororities aren't allowed to, but it's easy to have a very active social life without ever stepping foot in a frat house. I've found that a lot of the people who do choose to get involved **don't necessarily fit the usual stereotypes**, and even though it's not really my thing, I have some friends who have had very good experiences with them. Only about 14 to 15 percent of people pledge."

Q "I'm in a sorority, even though I didn't really intend on being a part of the Greek system before I came. It's pretty small and doesn't dominate the social scene, but it is the frats that offer most of the parties on campus, and **many non-Greek people come to the parties**."

Q "Frats don't dominate social life at all. **Sororities are kind of a joke here**. Freshman year, we were all big on going out to frats because you meet a lot of people, but now it's become a bit of a nuisance. There are parties to go elsewhere, and once you know upperclassmen, there's always another place to party."

Q "I've been to a frat house maybe three times this year, and two of the times we just watched football. **Freshmen tend to go to frat parties**, but that's about it."

### The College Prowler Take On...
# Greek Life

The nice thing about the Greek system at Tufts is that they are always looking for new members, so almost all Tufts students get to sample what the system is like through open parties and other events. The pressure to join isn't strong, and if you choose not to, you won't be excluded. If you decide that Greek Life is not your thing, don't fear. Greek life doesn't dominate the social scene; there are plenty of other options.

Recently, the administration has been cracking down on the Greek system in an attempt to add more unity, charity efforts, and safety to the system. Complaints about the administration trying to eliminate the Greek system are commonplace on campus. However, in the face of adversity, the community appears to be more unified than ever. Without a doubt, there will be major changes in the Greek system within the next few years, some for better, others for worse.

**The College Prowler® Grade on**

**Greek Life: C**

A high grade in Greek Life indicates that sororities and fraternities are not only present, but also active on campus. Other determining factors include the variety of houses available and the respect the Greek community receives from the rest of the campus.

# Drug Scene

The Lowdown On...
## Drug Scene

**Most Prevalent Drugs on Campus:**
Cocaine

Marijuana

**Liquor-Related Referrals:**
275

**Liquor-Related Arrests:**
1

**Drug-Related Referrals:**
77

**Drug-Related Arrests:**
0

## The Alcohol and Health Education Center

124 Professors Row

(617) 627-3861

Services: Addiction counseling, alcohol and drug-free social events, counseling and psychiatric services, discussion groups, leadership opportunities such as Peer Education and Campus and Community Advisory Council, Medical Care and Assessment, newsletter, peer support groups, Prevention Education, Outreach & Training Program, support for family members and children of addicts, treatment referral and information

## Drug Counseling Programs

The Tufts University Counseling Center
Sawyer House
(617) 353-3360
*http://ase.tufts.edu/counselingcenter*

The Danielson Institute
185 Bay State Rd.
(617) 353-3047

Student Health/Mental Health Services
881 Commonwealth Ave.
(617) 353-3030

Students Speak Out On...
# Drug Scene

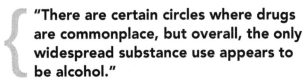

{ **"There are certain circles where drugs are commonplace, but overall, the only widespread substance use appears to be alcohol."**

Q "There probably are drugs, but I have **never seen or heard about them** on campus."

Q "If your thing is drugs, and you're from the West Coast, **prepare for a little culture shock**. A lot of people don't do drugs at Tufts, so the scene is really limited to a few groups who pretty much all know each other."

Q "I think the drug scene is existent, but **not overwhelming**."

Q "Drugs go around without dominating the social scene. **There aren't that many serious users** here, but most drugs are available, if desired."

Q "There's **lots of beer and weed**, and you can easily find anything else you want, but drugs don't dominate at all."

Q "Pot is very big, as is ecstasy. **I hear about acid and coke**, but I've never seen it done, and I've never encountered anything."

Q "I don't find drugs to be very prominent, but I guess it all depends on **who you choose to hang out with**."

Q "Drugs are available if you want them, like on any campus, but they're by no means prevalent. The same with drinking—you can if you want, but **nobody will think any less of you if you don't**."

Q "Druggies manage to keep themselves away from people that don't want them to be there, if that makes sense. People into the scene usually hang out with other people that are into it, and **they do a good job of hiding their problem**. That's right, I said 'problem.'"

Q "If you want to do drugs, you can get them, but if you don't want to do them, **there's not a lot of pressure**. I lived in a frat house and never felt any. Just be your own person, and do what you want to do."

# The College Prowler Take On...
# Drug Scene

One thing's for sure, there isn't any social pressure to do drugs at Tufts. As a matter of fact, a student here could very well go their entire college career without seeing anything more than alcohol and cigarettes. However, this isn't to say that Tufts University is a modern-day Pleasantville, either. Generally, where there is smoking and drinking, marijuana isn't far away; there are also a few rich fraternity boys here and there that are known for their coke habits.

Overall, though, there aren't a lot of chain smokers or coke users on campus, though alcohol and marijuana are somewhat prevalent. The average Tufts student will probably drink on weekends and smoke from time to time, but as for the drug scene, there is virtually nothing to worry about. There's no need to use anything to fit in. In fact, the crowds that do use illegal substances are mostly isolated from the rest of the student body.

### The College Prowler® Grade on
## Drug Scene: B+

A high grade in the Drug Scene indicates that drugs are not a noticeable part of campus life; drug use is not visible, and no pressure to use them seems to exist.

# Campus Strictness

**The Lowdown On...**
## Campus Strictness

### What Are You Most Likely to Get Caught Doing on Campus?

- Smoking or drinking in a dorm room
- Parking illegally

Students Speak Out On...
# Campus Strictness

"The police seem pretty relaxed, but that's because the scene is not really an issue. If parties begin to bother other people or look potentially dangerous, then police will step in. The worst I've heard happening is a $100 fine."

Q "Police have an observation-type policy about drinking, where they usually just let everyone leave broken-up parties without a problem. **If you get sick, though, you will get reported** and get 'Disciplinary Probation I' (a warning). Other than that, there's not a whole lot else to say."

Q "The campus police tend to be pretty lenient about students partying. **The police normally don't interrupt parties until about 2 a.m.** And if they catch students drinking underage, they will just give them a warning. But as long as students are not being disruptive while drinking, the police don't get involved."

Q "**Don't let them catch you with drugs**—they aren't trying to catch anybody because it's bad press. Likewise, they only bother about drinking if they have no choice, like if you are so drunk that you need medical attention. Parties get broken up at 2 a.m., though."

Q "Tufts police **don't really have too much to do**, so they spend their time being annoying with parking tickets. The police will break up parties if people get too rowdy, but they're generally pretty cool."

Q "It really depends on where you live. If you live in the dorms, you have to be careful of **RAs who will write you up** if they catch you. That will only happen if you are being very loud and stupid. If you live anywhere else, it is unlikely you will get into trouble if you are with a small number of people. Police only get involved in large gatherings."

Q "Police make sure everyone is safe. If you get caught, you aren't automatically kicked out of school—**you just get put on probation**, which isn't a big deal."

Q "The police are pretty lenient. A lot of the time, they begin **busting frat parties** when it starts getting late, but you don't normally get in trouble for drinking if you're underage, unless you get caught by police drinking outside. Even then, you only get on Probation I, which is only like a warning. The same goes if you are caught smoking pot, but that doesn't normally happen unless someone complains about it. For Probation II, I think they tell your parents, and then on Probation III, you're gone. I never got Probation I, and I was caught drinking a few times."

Q "The past two years, the police have been a little stricter with the party scene, but only because of several hazing episodes at places like MIT and University of Michigan. Though nothing happened at Tufts, it's caused college campuses to really **buckle down on their policy**. Lately, the police have eased up a little, and I'm sure they'll be a little more lenient in the upcoming years."

### The College Prowler Take On...
# Campus Strictness

The campus police and RAs don't enjoy busting people for a couple of beer cans in their dorm room, but if you are stupid about it, and people can hear what is going on in your room from far away, you aren't really leaving them any choice. When the policies are enforced, they can be quite strict, so once you are on probation, it's best to be super-careful. The consequences are severe if you get caught doing anything else while on probation. Overall, however, authorities at Tufts are more lenient than many of the colleges in the city.

The police and the fraternities have (unofficially) reached a general agreement about how to keep parties safe and under control; police will usually just sit outside a party to make sure nothing crazy or out-of-hand happens. Students, generally, view the police as harmless, helpful individuals rather than angry and irritated authority figures. The police seem to be more concerned with handing out parking tickets than anything else. Many parties are broken up at 2 a.m., which can put a damper on the night, but the good side to this is that arrests and referrals are uncommon.

**The College Prowler® Grade on**

**Campus Strictness: B+**

A high Campus Strictness grade implies an overall lenient atmosphere; police and RAs are fairly tolerant, and the administration's rules are flexible.

# Parking

### The Lowdown On...
## Parking

**Student Parking Lot?**
Yes

**Approximate Parking Permit Cost:**
$440 for full-time parking for one year, $220 for commuter parking

**Freshmen Allowed to Park?**
No (though exceptions may be granted)

**Common Parking Tickets:**
No Parking Zone: $15
Handicapped Zone: $50 (and usually towing fees)
No Decal: $50

## Tufts Parking Services

TUPD Administrative Services

419 Boston Avenue

Medford, MA 02155

(617) 627-3692

parking@tufts.edu

## Somerville Traffic and Parking

133 Holland St., Davis Square

(617) 625-6600 ext. 7900

## Parking Permits

Talk to TUPD at the beginning of the year to purchase a parking decal. The parking permit is definitely worth it because the ticket prices are so high, but you can always take your chances. To apply for a decal, you must present your valid Tufts ID and the vehicle registration. Students with vehicles registered out of state must provide proof of vehicle insurance. If you buy a parking pass, they will absolve your tickets for that semester. Make sure to put the parking decal on the left side window, so that you don't have to deal with the hassle of getting ticketed by accident.

## Did You Know?

### Best Places to Find a Parking Spot

Cousens Lot

South Lot

### Good Luck Finding a Spot Here!

Carmichael Lot

Latin Way Strip

### Students Speak Out On...
# Parking

**"Parking can get crowded at certain times, and can be expensive, but the ticketing system is pretty lax, so you can get by with a lot."**

Q "**Parking at Tufts is really easy**. There are parking lots everywhere. It is kind of expensive, but totally worth it."

Q "You can usually find parking **on the streets around the campus**, maybe even look into getting a Somerville parking pass through a friend's off-campus house address."

Q "**Parking is tough around the dorms**, and can sometimes be a huge hassle. There's no parking around a lot of the academic buildings, and the on-campus parking passes are kind of expensive. If you don't have a parking pass, tickets are $50; when you get 7 of those, your car is towed for a high price."

Q "**Parking is fine if you get a permit**, which isn't that expensive. If you don't, it's tickets galore! There are lots of places to park on campus if you have a permit, though."

Q "Freshmen aren't allowed to have a car on campus, though, they built a new garage to free up more parking on campus, and allow more sophomores on-campus spots. There is **a giant lot near the football field** called Cousen's Lot that you can buy a pass for, but it's about a three to five minute walk from campus."

Q "It's easy to park, but **freshmen can't have cars**. You need a very cheap parking permit, but then it's not a problem."

Q "You can't have a car on campus as a freshman, at least not legally. You can park it off campus, but then you'll probably get a ticket, or have trouble finding a place. It's a crowded area. You can have a car after freshman year, but **parking is a little bit of a problem**."

Q "Parking is not easy, though, it's gotten a lot better since they built the parking garage. Use the car for off-campus travels—**you can walk to everything on campus**."

Q "It is much easier to park as an upperclassman. I think you can get a **$220 pass per semester**. Honestly, the campus is not that big, and it's in an urban area, so having a car is not really necessary. There is also a shuttle and train access, which makes getting around much easier. I did not have a car until senior year, and I did fine."

Q "No cars for freshmen, but there is really no need. We are on the subway, and it's only a dollar. **Parking in Boston is expensive**, and traffic stinks."

Q "The campus is small enough that most people just walk, and I know of no one who drives to classes. Cars are helpful to move around outside of Boston, but the T (the subway system here) is the way to go. **Take it from me, a New Jersey driver**, that you do not want to drive in Boston."

# The College Prowler Take On...
# Parking

While driving in downtown Boston can be a bit disheartening, having a car on campus can be beneficial to students because it reduces travel time, and adds a lot of convenience to grocery shopping. Parking can be difficult, however, and with three separate police departments all ready to ticket, the costs can add up quick if you leave your car somewhere you shouldn't. If you think you'll need to travel outside of the Boston area, a car can be indispensable; for getting in and out of the city, however, public transit is generally quicker, and tends to be less nerve-racking.

It's almost impossible to find parking close to the dorms, especially around noon when the campus is full of people, but there are plenty of empty spots in the Cousen's lot. It's a short walk from the rest of campus, but you won't really need it to get to class anyway. Students generally agree that the parking decal is worth it, despite the hefty fee—being able to leave your car in the lots or garages without worrying about constant $50 tickets is a huge plus. Eventually, these do show up on your bursar's bill, and your mom and dad won't be too happy.

**The College Prowler® Grade on**

Parking: C-

A high grade in this section indicates that parking is both available and affordable, and that parking enforcement isn't overly severe.

# Transportation

### The Lowdown On...
## Transportation

### Ways to Get Around Town:

#### On Campus
Tufts' campus shuttle—with service uphill, downhill, and to Davis Square.

#### Public Transportation
Massachusetts Bay Transportation Authority—buses and the T. See *www.mbta.com* for schedules.

### Taxi Cabs
Yellow/Green Cab
(617) 628-0600
(617) 625-5000

Tan Cab
(781) 396-7777

### Car Rentals
Alamo
national: (800) 327-9633
*www.alamo.com*

**(Car Rentals, continued)**

Avis, local: (617) 534-1420
national: (800) 831-2847
*www.avis.com*

Budget, local: (781) 396-0776
national: (800) 527-0700
*www.budget.com*

Dollar, local: (617) 723-8312
national: (800) 800-4000
*www.dollar.com*

Enterprise,
local: (781) 391-1561
national: (800) 736-8222
*www.enterprise.com*

Hertz, local: (781) 306-0610
national: (800) 654-3131
*www.hertz.com*

National, local: (617) 557-7179
national: (800) 227-7368
*www.nationalcar.com*

**Best Ways to Get Around Town**

Bus

The T

Walk

# Ways to Get Out of Town:

### Airport

Logan International Airport
(800) 23-LOGAN
*www.massport.com/logan*

### Airlines Serving Boston

Aer Lingus
(888) 474-7424
*www.aerlingus.ie*

**(Airlines Serving Boston, continued)**

Air Canada (888) 247-2262
*www.aircanada.ca*

Air France (800) 237-2747
*www.airfrance.com*

Air Jamaica (800) 523-3515
*www.airjamaica.com*

Air Tran (800) 247-8726
*www.airtran.com*

Alaska Airlines (800) 252-7522
*www.alaskaair.com*

Alitalia (800) 223-5730
*www.alitalia.it*

America West (800) 235-9292
*www.americawest.com*

American Eagle (800) 433-7300
*www.aa.com*

American Trans Air
(800) 225-2995
*www.ata.com*

British Airways (800) 247-9297
*www.british-airways.com*

Cape Air (800) 352-0714
*www.flycapeair.com*

Charters (617) 634-6270

Continental (800) 525-0280
*www.continental.com*

Delta Air Lines (800) 221-1212
*www.delta.com*

Icelandair (800) 223-5500
*www.icelandair.com*

KLM (800) 374-7747
*www.klm.com*

Lufthansa (800) 645-3880
*www.lufthansa.com*

Midwest Express
(800) 452-2022
*www.midwestexpress.com*

## (Airlines Serving Boston, continued)

Northwest (800) 225-2525
*www.nwa.com*

Swiss (877) 359-7947
*www.swiss.com*

United Airlines (800) 241-6522
*www.ual.com*

US Airways (800) 428-4322
*www.usairways.com*

Virgin Atlantic (800) 862-8621
*www.virginatlantic.com*

## How to Get to the Airport

The Turkey/Holiday Shuttle offered from campus directly to Logan.

Take the T. The airport stop is on the blue line.

Driving: Take Highway I-93 South. Follow downtown signs until you see signs for the Callahan Tunnel/Logan Airport. At the bottom of the ramp, turn left into the Callahan Tunnel. After exiting the tunnel, stay right; the second exit is the airport access road.

A cab ride to the airport costs around $25

## Greyhound

The Greyhound Bus Station is located at the South Station terminal's multilevel bus deck. For schedule information call Greyhound at (800) 229-9424 or visit *www.greyhound.com.*

Greyhound Bus Station, Boston
South Station

Atlantic Ave. and Summer St.
Boston, MA 02110

(617) 222-3200

## Amtrak

The closest Amtrak station to Tufts is South Station, in the center of Boston. You can take the T directly from Davis Square to South Station.

For schedule information, call (800) 872-7245, or visit *www.amtrak.com.*

Amtrak South Station (BOS), Boston

Atlantic Ave. and Summer St.
Boston, MA 02110

(617) 222-3200

**Travel Agents**

Mystic Valley Travel Inc.
15 Salem St., Medford
(781) 396-0710

MTL Vacations
100 Cummings Center
Suite 120, Beverly
(978) 998-6013
*www.mtlvacations.com*

US Travel World
660 Broadway, Somerville
(617) 776-4444

Cambridge Travel Inc.
Porter Square Galleria,
1 Porter Square Street,
Cambridge
(617) 491-3800

### Students Speak Out On...
# Transportation

> "Around Medford, there is no public transit. It's great to get into the Boston core, but if you want to go in any other direction on a regular basis, look into bringing your car."

Q "The subway is really close, and **it takes only 15 minutes to get downtown**. It's just a buck to go anywhere in the city, and it's the best way to go. Campus is also served by a few bus routes, which are under-utilized, and provide quick service into Cambridge and the nearby shopping mall."

Q "The T can get you around Boston. **The T stop is only a 10-to-15-minute walk from Tufts**. However, the T closes at about 12:30 a.m. Also, the T is a good way to get to the center of Boston, but if you want to go anywhere else, the T takes forever. Having a car makes getting to places much more convenient."

Q "The shuttle is okay; **it seems to take forever**, and the random stopping at the Campus Center for 20 minutes is frustrating. Other than that, it's good. I like the variety of stops (though, I don't enjoy people taking advantage of that and asking to stop everywhere on campus)."

Q "The T makes having a car completely unnecessary. It is sometimes slow, but **very accessible** from all over the city."

Q "You have to take a shuttle to get to the T (the subway), which can be a bit inconvenient, but **they have more cars circulating now**."

Q "Public transportation is the way to go in every instance. Boston's a busy city, and cars definitely are not convenient. The subway is **the best way to get around**, and it branches out to all of Boston and its surrounding areas."

Q "The subway is very convenient. There's a shuttle that runs from **campus to Davis square**, which is a stop on the 'red line.' Also on the 'red line' are Harvard, MIT, and South Station, where you can catch a train or bus to go basically anywhere in the country. The subway connects to all other parts of Boston, making everything really accessible. There's also a system of bus routes that cover almost all of Boston, and the buses run right through Tufts, too."

Q "**Transportation is excellent**. The shuttle takes us from campus to the main square. The subway can be a pain to wait for, and sometimes it's easier to walk to Davis, the main square, but the T is better and cleaner than the New York subway lines."

## The College Prowler Take On...
# Transportation

Though a good majority of Tufts students bring cars to campus, many agree that they don't really need to. Boston has amazing public transportation, and the T is not only super-affordable ($1.25 per ride), but it takes you almost anyplace you would ever have to go in the Boston area. The bus is even cheaper than the T, but it's not nearly as reliable—driving is preferable to the bus route any day.

A car is good if you need to go somewhere that isn't on the T, and if you live off campus, it becomes very convenient for grocery runs. Don't worry about having to walk to and from the parking lots; Boston is a very pretty city, which makes walking that much more enjoyable, and Tufts' hill will enable you to graduate with rock-solid calves. Tufts also offers airport transportation shuttles and other services designed to make things easier for students. The campus safety shuttle, dubbed the "Joey," is a good way to get around, and you can even take it up the hill to class if you're feeling extraordinarily lazy. Overall, students are generally satisfied with the quality of transportation in town, and it does allow them a lot of independence.

**B+**

The College Prowler® Grade on
### Transportation: B+

A high grade for Transportation indicates that campus buses, public buses, cabs and rental cars are readily available and affordable. Other determining factors include proximity to an airport and the necessity of transportation.

# Weather

The Lowdown On...
## Weather

**Average Temperature:**

| | |
|---|---|
| Fall: | 51°F |
| Winter: | 25°F |
| Spring: | 46°F |
| Summer: | 71°F |

**Average Precipitation:**

| | |
|---|---|
| Fall: | 3.67 in. |
| Winter: | 3.98 in. |
| Spring: | 3.70 in. |
| Summer: | 3.13 in |

## Students Speak Out On...
# Weather

"It gets very cold! I hate the cold! You get used to it, though, and it looks absolutely beautiful when a blanket of snow covers the campus. Spring and fall are very pleasant seasons, and the campus looks great."

Q "It's Boston; it's cold as ever. Be prepared for one of the worst, **most miserable winters of your life** if you're from anywhere south. October weather will probably depress you, let alone February."

Q "The snow can begin to get to you after months of cold. Definitely **pack sledding/snowball-fighting clothes**! You'll want them for the first big snowfall. You should have a good pair of waterproof shoes, and definitely an umbrella."

Q "Being from a much sunnier state, it was cool to see snow for the first time, but it got old fast. I did make **some pretty fancy snowmen**, though!"

Q "**It's unbearably freezing in the winter**, hot and humid in the late fall, and then second spring begins because it is late every year, around when we take finals, and then we leave and go somewhere else for the summer."

Q "The weather is the only negative part of Tufts. It gets cold, and we don't get hot weather again until April, but I am from Miami, and I survived very well through the winter. As long as you have warm clothes, **the weather is tolerable**."

Q "It's **typical New England weather**, with four distinct seasons and a pretty cold, snowy winter

Q "It's New England, and **it'll change in a second**. Bring every kind of clothing—we had a couple snow days freshman year, but by the time we moved out in May, it was in the 90s."

Q "The first winter took some getting used to, but it's no sweat by now. **Even my friends from LA can tough it out** now without too much complaining—and spring and fall are really nice."

Q "The weather is typical New England weather. It rains a fair amount, and winter lasts a long time. But if it snows in the winter, **it's really fun to go sledding around campus**. And springtime is really pretty. Definitely bring clothes for the winter, but also for fall and spring. Winter averages are 20 to 30 degrees. Fall and spring are about 60 degrees."

Q "The weather is horrible, **absolutely horrible**. If you've lived in a warmer climate all your life, you will be so depressed. Trust me."

Q "We get a gorgeous fall and late spring, but in between it stinks. It gets cold and rainy, and then it'll become inexplicably sunny, oftentimes within a 21-hour period. **It's not too muggy** like it can be further south, but it gets pretty warm during the summer."

Q "I love New England weather—**it's so seasonal**. No weather has ever prevented me from going out. Snow days are awesome, and the campus is not too big to have to brave the elements sometimes."

Q "During school, you get great weather right when you start and right when you end. Sometimes, there's a lot of snow during the winter, and **the fall is beautiful in Boston**—it's quite a sight to see!"

### The College Prowler Take On...
# Weather

Tufts is in New England, so you're going to get weather from all seasons. It is really hot from May to August, extraordinarily rainy in March and April, and pretty much cold and snowy the rest of the year. Fall semester, it will snow probably just a few times, but despite the name, "spring" semester is much, much colder, and students will return to campus to see it covered in snow. Don't be surprised to see it snowing in April and May.

The good news is that the campus is so beautiful that all seasons are pleasant (to an extent, of course), even if they're not always comfortable. If you are looking for warm weather year round, obviously Tufts isn't for you. To survive, a sense of humor about the weather is all it takes. Feel free to make jokes about the occasional floods from all the rain, or how Tufts is too cheap to air condition the dorms; and if it snows, feel free to grab a sled, a dining hall tray, or even your roomate's mattress, and go sledding down the President's Lawn!

**The College Prowler® Grade on**

### Weather: C-

A high Weather grade designates that temperatures are mild and rarely reach extremes, that the campus tends to be sunny rather than rainy, and that weather is fairly consistent rather than unpredictable.

TUFTS UNIVERSITY

# Report Card Summary

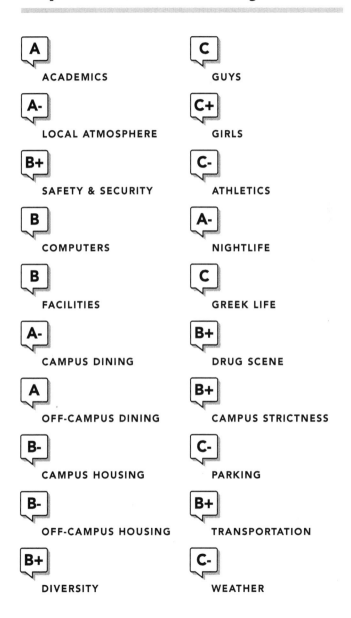

**A**
ACADEMICS

**C**
GUYS

**A-**
LOCAL ATMOSPHERE

**C+**
GIRLS

**B+**
SAFETY & SECURITY

**C-**
ATHLETICS

**B**
COMPUTERS

**A-**
NIGHTLIFE

**B**
FACILITIES

**C**
GREEK LIFE

**A-**
CAMPUS DINING

**B+**
DRUG SCENE

**A**
OFF-CAMPUS DINING

**B+**
CAMPUS STRICTNESS

**B-**
CAMPUS HOUSING

**C-**
PARKING

**B-**
OFF-CAMPUS HOUSING

**B+**
TRANSPORTATION

**B+**
DIVERSITY

**C-**
WEATHER

# Overall Experience

**Students Speak Out On...**
## Overall Experience

> { "I like Tufts—even with its flaws. The school is growing, and it's nice to be a part of that. I wish we had better race relations, more school spirit, and a bigger endowment. But I feel like I'm getting a real world education."

> ◯ "I always thought that people who wanted to transfer hadn't really learned enough about Tufts yet. If you **give Tufts a chance** and get involved, there isn't really much you would dislike enough to make you want to leave. Tufts is a wonderful place, and I feel like I've really gotten a quality education here."

Q "I'm really happy at Tufts. Sometimes, I wonder what would have happened if I went somewhere else, but I definitely feel that **I made the right choice**. I really like my friends, classes, and profs. Overall, it's been a good experience."

Q "**All around, Tufts is a solid school**. It doesn't have a lot going for it that would make you jump up and down in joy, but if you get involved, there's no reason you shouldn't have a good time and meet a lot of cool people. I'm glad I came to Tufts, although I kind of wish there was more of a character to the place, but that's tough when you're in a suburb. A lot of people like Tufts because it's just outside the city, but I'd rather be right in the center of things. It's a small place, so be prepared to know everybody, but it's big enough that you shouldn't feel claustrophobic."

Q "I play varsity field hockey and sing in an a cappella group, and both of those groups really made my first-year experience amazing. **Extracurriculars are huge at Tufts**—there's something for everyone, from the Tufts' Dance Collective to a society that discusses Simpsons episodes. Honestly, I haven't met any freshmen who didn't love their first year, and couldn't wait to go back."

Q "Tufts is truly **a unique place**. Most people who go here love it, and I think that defends Tufts against its previous reputation of being the Ivy reject school."

Q "**I used to wish I were somewhere else**, but not any more. I have been through many great things at Tufts and have had met many wonderful people. I even got to go to Cuba! College is definitely what you make of it, no matter where you go. Just be open-minded about things, and make sure that you look for the good things as opposed to the bad. When I did that, I saw that I was at a great school with a great reputation, and that it has a lot to offer me."

Q "I love Tufts. **I had trouble adjusting as a freshman**, but now I have met amazing people, and I'm doing really well."

Q "**I'd advise going anywhere but Tufts**, or you'll regret it. I actually left Tufts last year, and I am going to UCLA as a junior this fall. I was pretty miserable after my first year—a popular sentiment among the students, especially those from the West Coast."

Q "**I have zero regrets**—I love Tufts. I would probably have had a great time anywhere, after a slightly negative high school experience. It kind of stunk going cross-coast, as now I'm nowhere near any of my old friends, but it was great to experience another part of the country."

Q "**Coming to Tufts was one of the best decisions I've ever made**. Enough said."

Q "**People are always impressed** when I tell them I went to Tufts. It's got a great reputation, and our new president is awesome. I will miss my years at Tufts. You go to college to find out what kind of person you are, and in my opinion, Tufts allowed me to do that."

Q "College is basically what you make of it, and at Tufts **you have access to whatever** you want to do."

### The College Prowler Take On...
# Overall Experience

Most students who made the decision to attend Tufts are happy with their experience. Overall, Tufts has so many programs and activities, it's impossible for one student to take advantage of everything the school has to offer in four short years, but since there are so many different types of students at Tufts, all with different interests, there is definitely something for everyone. The biggest complaint coming from the students seems to be adjusting to the new lifestyle and environment, whether at the school itself, or the Boston area in general.

The Tufts experience goes far beyond the classroom, and provides students easy access to the ideal academic and social surroundings. The combination of school opportunities and local culture give Tufts its own distinctive flavor that allows students to grow in ways they never could have imagined. Most of the negative experiences that Tufts students gripe about are also good growth experiences (dealing with the weather, or actually having to get around without a car). Ultimately, graduates are proud of their education and their school. Students who graduate from Tufts enter the real world focused, confident, and prepared to face even the toughest challenges that the workplace can throw at them. The many successful Tufts alumni can attest to this.

# The Inside Scoop

**The Lowdown On...**
## The Inside Scoop

### Tufts Slang:

Know the slang, know the school. The following is a list of things you really need to know before coming to TU. The more of these words you know, the better off you'll be.

**A Cappella** – Singing without accompaniment.

**CSL** – Committee on Student Life.

**Dewick** – When going to eat at Dewick, someone may ask you, "Do you want to Dewick it?"

**Double-Jumbo** – Someone who has attended Tufts both as an undergraduate and graduate, or professional student.

**Downhill** – Using the library steps as the dividing line.

**E** – Short for "Engineer."

**ELBO** – Elections Board.

**Ex College** – Experimental College, a program that brings in outside experts to teach classes.

**Flip Cup** – A drinking game played by two teams. The game proceeds as a relay.

**Jackson College** – The name of the Tufts' college for women (from before the University became coed).

**JumboFOB** – Electronic signal keys used to enter some dorms.

**Light on the Hill** – A number of school traditions and songs derive from this phrase that initiated Tufts' creation, when Nathan Tufts vowed "to put a light on the hill."

**O-zone** – Where you live if you're on the basement level of a dorm.

**Pax Et Lux** – Latin for "Peace and Light," and is part of the Tufts symbol.

**P-Row** – Professors Row.

**Quad** – Area of grass surrounded on all sides by buildings.

**TCU** – Tufts Community Union; student government groups, TCU Senate, and Judiciary.

**TEMS** – Tufts Emergency Medical Service, the group of student-EMTs on call for emergency service.

**The Hill** – Walnut Hill, where Tufts is located.

**Uphill** – Using the library steps as the dividing line.

**Wren Bugs** – The special species of bugs that live in and around Wren Hall.

## Things I Wish I Knew Before Coming to Tufts

- Go to office hours and ask a lot of questions.

- Do not try to do everything on your own, sometimes you need help.

- Fill your math requirement freshman year.

- Do not dedicate your whole life to one activity right away, and shop around for a year before becoming super-involved.

- Bring your own computer.

- Get the 160-meal plan, always, until you have your own kitchen.

- Go to the frat parties during orientation week—they are the best parties all year, especially ZBT's jello shots.

## Tips to Succeed at Tufts

- Get involved in an organization, and rise to a leadership role.
- Go to office hours so some professors will know you well.
- Learn to write well.
- If a professor is bad, don't stick around. Drop the class, and switch into something that will keep you interested.
- Check e-mail constantly.
- Don't even try to apply for an on-campus apartment before you are a senior, unless a senior is pulling you into an apartment.
- Study abroad so that you don't have to deal with finding junior-year housing.
- Look for sophomore-year housing in older dorms, or Tufts-owned houses—they have the biggest rooms.
- First semester, take courses in very different subjects so you can find out what you like.
- Write a senior thesis even though you don't have to.

## Tufts Urban Legends

### Direction of the Tufts Cannon

There is a replica of a U.S.S. Constitution cannon on the Tufts campus. It is said it points at Harvard, but no one really knows where it points.

### Jumbo

If you can get a penny to land on the nose of the Jumbo statue, you're supposed to have good luck on your finals.

### Rape Steps

These steps are behind the Hillel Center and lead down to Boston Avenue. They say that the design of these steps was given to an engineering student as his final project. He was supposed to design them so that they would be easier for women to run up than men if they were being chased, and the steps were designed to be the exact stride of a woman, calculated from a number of biological factors. However, an empirical study will show that men can run up these steps twice as fast as women. The stride length is difficult for women, but men can just jump two steps at a time.

## School Color Selection

In the first 30 years of Tufts's existence, the graduating class was allowed to pick their own school colors, and every year they changed. After 30 years, the administration decided it was time to settle on one set of colors. When the administration told the senior class that they would pick the school's colors for eternity, they didn't believe them, and thought it was a joke. That class picked the worst color combination they could come up with: baby blue and dark brown. Those remain Tufts' colors today. Tufts says the school colors represent earth and sky.

## Wren Bugs

This is a unique species of bug that supposedly only inhabits Wren Hall. No one has seen much of them lately, and they may have been exterminated, or at least gone into hiding.

# School Spirit

Students will go to Homecoming and Parents' weekend football games, and if a team is doing really well, they will get excited about it; but Tufts school spirit extends further than sports. Despite the name sounding bad at first, almost all Tufts students are proud to be Jumbos. Most Tufts students express an affinity for Jumbo, and could recite the story of how Jumbo came to be Tufts' mascot, and of the tragic fire that destroyed the real Jumbo. Most students are very happy at Tufts, and proud of their school. In times of tragedy, the campus is able to come together very quickly and support each other as members of a community. No one knows the alma mater except the a cappella groups, and most students could only mutter a few syllables of the fight song, but on Tuftonia's Day (Tufts' birthday), everyone celebrates. School spirit is hard to avoid, since the Tufts Spirit Coalition is always cooking up something.

# Traditions

## Candle Ceremonies
There is a big candle-lighting ceremony during Freshman Orientation and Senior Week. The traditions are derived from the Nathan Tufts vow to "put a light on the hill."

## First Night
The first night of Freshman Orientation, the entire class and A=alumni gather in the Gantcher Center for dinner and the story of Jumbo. Watch out for indoor fireworks.

## Frisbee Golf
Watch out for flying Frisbees! There is a Frisbee golf course on campus, and it is only known to members of the ultimate Frisbee team. They aren't trying to hit you in the head with the Frisbee, they just want it to land on Jumbo's nose.

## Naked Quad Run
In the 1960s, students who were living in West Hall (the last all-male dorm on campus) were told that women would be moving in the next year, and they decided to protest. They ran naked around the academic quad, and it has been a tradition ever since. The event traditionally takes place on the first night of reading period in December, usually with some amount of snow on the ground.

## Pancake Breakfast
This used to happen after the Naked Quad Run, but now due to a number of incidents with naked pancake throwing, the event has been moved to a study break during reading period in the spring semester.

## Painting the Cannon
This is the best form of advertising on campus. Every night, students are allowed to paint the cannon, though painting may only be done in the dark. Students then guard the cannon until dawn. If you don't, it is free-game to anyone else to paint over.

# Finding a Job or Internship

### The Lowdown On...
## Finding a Job or Internship

Career Services probably won't be very helpful in actually putting you in contact with someone who could find you a job, but they do provide a number of workshops throughout your four years. Junior and senior year workshops have particularly good information on how to beef up your resumé, interview for a job, and focus your skills toward various sectors of the economy. Career Services is also very helpful with finding internships, and you can set up an appointment at any time to go over a cover letter or resume. A lot of students will do summer internships, and even internships during the semester, and Tufts has a lot of connections in Boston that can help students find out about these opportunities. There are a few internships for credit, but check with a department before you start looking so you know what you can get credit for.

## Advice

- Look for an internship well in advance. Some of the best internships have deadlines in November.

- Have Career Services read over your cover letter and resume. They know what they're talking about.

- Look through all the information on the Web, such as the Tufts Career Network and E-recruiting; these are all accessible from the career services Web site.

- Go to career fairs. Even if there is nothing you're interested in, at least you'll get a better handle on the job market and networking skills.

## Career Center Resources and Services

Tufts University
419 Boston Ave.
Dowling Hall, Suite 740
Medford, MA 02155

(617) 627-3299

career.services@ase.tufts.edu

*http://careers.tufts.edu*

# Alumni

**The Lowdown On...**
## Alumni

**Web Site:**
*www.tufts.edu/alumni*

**Alumni Office:**
Office of Alumni Relations
95 Talbot Avenue
Medford, MA 02155
(617) 627-3532
(800) THE-ALUM

**Services Available:**
Alumni directory
Alumni e-mail
Alumni gatherings
Career services
Credit card
Local chapters
Merchandise
Tufts online community

**Alumni Publication:**
*Tufts Magazine*

## Major Alumni Events

**Alumni Weekend** – Tufts alumni all come back to campus at the same time for 5-year, 10-year, and 25-year reunions. These coincide with commencement.

**Homecoming** – A chance for alumni of all ages to come back to the hill and hang out with organizations they were once a part of.

**Reunion Dinners** – These happen throughout the year, and provide a chance for local alumni to see each other.

*Tufts Magazine* – All graduates receive four free issues of *Tufts Magazine* each year to keep them tuned in with life on the hill.

**Tufts Night at the Pops** – One night out of the year, The Boston Pops play only for people affiliated with Tufts. This takes place during Alumni Weekend, and is a favorite event.

### Did You Know?

**Famous Tufts Alumni**

**Hank Azaria** – Actor

**Rob Burnett** – Creator of the TV show *Ed*

**Tracy Chapman** – Singer

**Pierre Omidyar** – E-bay founder

**Bill Richardson** – New Mexico Governor

# Student Organizations

## Academic

Biology Society

Math Club

Tau Beta Pi

## Cultural/Religious

African Student Organization

Arab Student Association

Armenian Club

Asian Christian Fellowship

Asian Community at Tufts

Association of Latin American Students (ALAS)

Bahai Association

Black Men's Group

Buddhist Sangha at Tufts

Caribbean Club

Catholic Community at Tufts

Chinese Student Association

## (Cultural/Religious, continued)

Chinese Students and Scholars Association

Filipino Cultural Society

Hawaii Club

Hellenic Society

Hillel

Hong Kong Students Association

Indian Society at Tufts

International Club

Italian Club

Japanese Culture Club

Korean Students Association (KSA)

Middle Eastern Student Society

Multiracial Organization of Students at Tufts

### (Cultural/Religious, continued)

Muslim Student Association

Orthodox Christian Fellowship

Pan-African Alliance

Protestant Student Fellowship

Puerto Rican Association

Russian Circle

Taiwanese Association of Students at Tufts

Thai Club

Tufts Association of South Asians

Tufts Christian Fellowship

Tufts Transgendered, Lesbian, Gay, Bisexual Collective

Turkish Student Association

Vietnamese Student Club

Women's Union at Tufts (WUT)

## Government/Political

American Civil Liberties Union

Amnesty International

Debate Society

Environmental Consciousness Outreach

Friends of Israel

Graduate Student Council

Students for the Ethical Treatment of Animals

Tufts Council of International Affairs

Tufts Democrats

Tufts Feminist Alliance

Tufts Republicans

Tufts Right to Arms

## Media

*Hemispheres*

Jumbo Audio Project

Media Advisory Board

*Observer*

*Onyx*

Optimus Prime

*Outbreath*

*Primary Source*

*South Asian Literary and Arts Magazine*

*Tufts Daily*

Tufts University Television

TuftScope

*TuftsLife.com*

WMFO 91.5FM

Yearbook

*Zamboni*

## Performance/Arts

Amalgamates (a capella)

Beats (Percussive Performance Group)

Chamber Singers

Cheap Sox

Chorale

Crafts Center

Explosion Latina Dance Troupe

HYPE Mime Group

Institute for Better Anime

Jumbo Marching Band

Pen, Paint & Pretzels

Sarabande

Spirit of Color

Torn Ticket II

## (Performance/Arts, continued)

Traveling Treasure Trunk

Tufts Capoeira

Tufts Dance Collective

Tufts Symphony Orchestra

Tufts University Wind Ensemble

TURBO (Break Dancing Troupe)

## Pre-Professional

American Chemical Society

American Institute of Chemical Engineers (AIChE)

American Medical Student Association

American Society of Civil Engineers

American Society of Mechanical Engineers

Child Development Association

Economics Society

Human Factors and Ergonomics Society

Institute of Electrical & Electronics Engineers

Investment Club

Pre-Dental Society

Pre-Legal Society

Pre-Veterinary Society

Public Health at Tufts (PHAT)

Society of Women Engineers

Tufts Joint Operations

Tufts Student Resources

## Student Government

Elections Board (ELBO)

Tufts Community Union Judiciary (TCU-J)

Tufts Community Union Senate

# The Best
# & Worst

## The Ten **BEST** Things About Tufts

| | |
|---|---|
| **1** | The Library roof (you'll understand when you get here) |
| **2** | Getting to know your professors |
| **3** | A cappella |
| **4** | Spring Fling |
| **5** | Opportunities to do research |
| **6** | Free movies from film series |
| **7** | Sunday brunch at Dewick |
| **8** | Great guest speakers (i.e. two former U.S. Presidents) |
| **9** | Six miles from Boston, but with an isolated campus |
| **10** | Smart, talented, and passionate student body |

# The Ten **WORST** Things About Tufts

**1** Being referred to as "Jumbo" all the time

**2** Walking uphill to class

**3** Trying to make brown and blue match

**4** Parking tickets

**5** Elitists—students who have "something to prove"

**6** Disgusting freshman bathrooms

**7** Administration crackdown on Greek system

**8** Ethnic self-segregation

**9** Long, drawn out battles between campus liberals and conservatives

**10** The small endowment

# Visiting

The Lowdown On...
## Visiting

### Hotel Information:

**A Cambridge House Bed & Breakfast Inn**

2218 Massachusetts Ave., Cambridge

(617) 491-6300

*www.acambridgehouse.com*

Distance from Campus: 1.5 miles

Price Range: $109–$229

**Amerisuites Boston Medford**

116 Riverside Ave., Medford

(781) 395-8500

*www.amerisuites.com*

Distance from Campus: 0.7 miles

Price Range: $109–$199

**Holiday Inn**
30 Washington St., Somerville
(617) 628-1000
Distance from Campus:
3 miles
Price Range: $119–$250

**La Quinta**
23 Cummings St., Somerville
(617) 625-5300
http://2003.lq.com
Distance from Campus:
2.5 miles
Price Range: $115–$145

**Meacham Manor Bed
& Breakfast**
52 Meacham Rd., Somerville
www.meacham-manor.com
(617) 623-3985
Distance from Campus:
1 mile
Price Range: $70–$125

**Sheraton Commander**
16 Garden St., Cambridge
(617) 547-4800
www.sheratoncommander.com
Distance from Campus:
2.5 miles
Price Range: $99–$525

## Take a Campus Virtual Tour

http://admissions.tufts.edu/vtour

## To Schedule a Group Information Session or Tour

Call (617) 627-3170 to make a reservation for a group information session as soon as your plans are finalized. Sessions run about an hour long. All interviews are done by alumni interviewers in your area. You will be contacted about an interview shortly after the office has received your application, though interviews are not mandatory.

## Campus Tours

Campus tours are led by a Tufts student and are an hour long, and include a view of the campus facilities and landscape. For a listing of tour times, click on the "campus tours" icon on the admissions Web site at http://admissions.tufts.edu/visit.htm#Campus%20Tours.

## Overnight Visits

One-night overnight stays are typically available from mid-October through mid-November for high school seniors, and during the month of April for admitted students, including during the April Open House Program. Current Tufts students have volunteered to host prospective high school seniors in their residence hall rooms on a first-come, first-served basis during certain times of the year. Students are available to host Monday through Thursday nights. If you are interested, contact the admissions office or sign up through their Web site at *http://admissions.tufts.edu/connection*.

## Directions to Campus

### Driving from the North

- If you are approaching on Routes 1, 95, 128, or 93, take Route 93 south to Exit 32, Medford Square.
- From the exit ramp, take the first right off the traffic circle, which is Route 60 West.
- At the second set of lights, bear left on Main Street and take an immediate right on to Route 16 West.
- Continue on Route 16 for approximately one and a quarter miles.
- An athletic field will appear on your right.
- Bear left through the next traffic circle, and proceed up the hill on Powder House Boulevard.
- At the third traffic light, turn left onto Packard Avenue.
- You are now on the Tufts campus.

## Driving from the Northwest

- If you are approaching on Route 2 East, continue on Route 2 past the junction of Routes 2 and 95.
- If you are approaching on Route 3, take Route 95 south to Route 2 east (Exit 29A).
- At the junction of Routes 2 and 16, bear left through a full traffic light on Route 16 east.
- Take Route 16 east through two traffic lights.
- You will see blue signs on the right for Tufts University.
- Follow the blue signs, and take a sharp right up the hill on Powder House Boulevard.
- At the third traffic light, turn left onto Packard Avenue. You are now on the Tufts campus.

## Driving from the West or Southwest

- If you are approaching on Routes 90 (Massachusetts Turnpike) or 95, take Route 95 north to Route 2 east (Exit 29A).
- At the junction of Routes 2 and 16, bear left through a full traffic light on Route 16 east, and refer to directions driving from the northwest.

## Driving from the South or Boston

- If you are coming from the South, take Route 3 North to Route 93 North.
- If coming from Boston, take Route 93 North.
- If coming from the airport, follow signs to Route 93 via the Sumner Tunnel.
- Take Route 93 North to Exit 31, and refer to directions driving from the north.

# Words to Know

**Academic Probation** – A suspension imposed on a student if he or she fails to keep up with the school's minimum academic requirements. Those unable to improve their grades after receiving this warning can face dismissal.

**Beer Pong/Beirut** – A drinking game involving cups of beer arranged in a pyramid shape on each side of a table. The goal is to get a Ping-Pong ball into one of the opponent's cups by throwing the ball or hitting it with a paddle. If the ball lands in a cup, the opponent is required to drink the beer.

**Bid** – An invitation from a fraternity or sorority to 'pledge' (join) that specific house.

**Blue-Light Phone** – Brightly-colored phone posts with a blue light bulb on top. These phones exist for security purposes and are located at various outside locations around most campuses. In an emergency, a student can pick up one of these phones (free of charge) to connect with campus police or a security escort.

**Campus Police** – Police who are specifically assigned to a given institution. Campus police are typically not regular city officers; they are employed by the university in a full-time capacity.

**Club Sports** – A level of sports that falls somewhere between varsity and intramural. If a student is unable to commit to a varsity team but has a lot of passion for athletics, a club sport could be a better, less intense option. Even less demanding, intramural (IM) sports often involve no traveling and considerably less time.

**Cocaine** – An illegal drug. Also known as "coke" or "blow," cocaine often resembles a white crystalline or powdery substance. It is highly addictive and dangerous.

**Common Application** – An application with which students can apply to multiple schools.

**Course Registration** – The period of official class selection for the upcoming quarter or semester. Prior to registration, it is best to prepare several back-up courses in case a particular class becomes full. If a course is full, students can place themselves on the waitlist, although this still does not guarantee entry.

**Division Athletics** – Athletic classifications range from Division I to Division III. Division IA is the most competitive, while Division III is considered to be the least competitive.

**Dorm** – A dorm (or dormitory) is an on-campus housing facility. Dorms can provide a range of options from suite-style rooms to more communal options that include shared bathrooms. Most first-year students live in dorms. Some upperclassmen who wish to stay on campus also choose this option.

**Early Action** – An application option with which a student can apply to a school and receive an early acceptance response without a binding commitment. This system is becoming less and less available.

**Early Decision** – An application option that students should use only if they are certain they plan to attend the school in question. If a student applies using the early decision option and is admitted, he or she is required and bound to attend that university. Admission rates are usually higher among students who apply through early decision, as the student is clearly indicating that the school is his or her first choice.

**Ecstasy** – An illegal drug. Also known as "E" or "X," ecstasy looks like a pill and most resembles an aspirin. Considered a party drug, ecstasy is very dangerous and can be deadly.

**Ethernet** – An extremely fast Internet connection available in most university-owned residence halls. To use an Ethernet connection properly, a student will need a network card and cable for his or her computer.

**Fake ID** – A counterfeit identification card that contains false information. Most commonly, students get fake IDs with altered birthdates so that they appear to be older than 21 (and therefore of legal drinking age). Even though it is illegal, many college students have fake IDs in hopes of purchasing alcohol or getting into bars.

**Frosh** – Slang for "freshman" or "freshmen."

**Hazing** – Initiation rituals administered by some fraternities or sororities as part of the pledging process. Many universities have outlawed hazing due to its degrading, and sometimes dangerous, nature.

**Intramurals (IMs)** – A popular, and usually free, sport league in which students create teams and compete against one another. These sports vary in competitiveness and can include a range of activities—everything from billiards to water polo. IM sports are a great way to meet people with similar interests.

**Keg** – Officially called a half-barrel, a keg contains roughly 200 12-ounce servings of beer.

**LSD** – An illegal drug, also known as acid, this hallucinogenic drug most commonly resembles a tab of paper.

**Marijuana** – An illegal drug, also known as weed or pot; along with alcohol, marijuana is one of the most commonly-found drugs on campuses across the country.

**Major** –The focal point of a student's college studies; a specific topic that is studied for a degree. Examples of majors include physics, English, history, computer science, economics, business, and music. Many students decide on a specific major before arriving on campus, while others are simply "undecided" until declaring a major. Those who are extremely interested in two areas can also choose to double major.

**Meal Block** – The equivalent of one meal. Students on a meal plan usually receive a fixed number of meals per week. Each meal, or "block," can be redeemed at the school's dining facilities in place of cash. Often, a student's weekly allotment of meal blocks will be forfeited if not used.

**Minor** – An additional focal point in a student's education. Often serving as a complement or addition to a student's main area of focus, a minor has fewer requirements and prerequisites to fulfill than a major. Minors are not required for graduation from most schools; however some students who want to explore many different interests choose to pursue both a major and a minor.

**Mushrooms** – An illegal drug. Also known as "'shrooms," this drug resembles regular mushrooms but is extremely hallucinogenic.

**Off-Campus Housing** – Housing from a particular landlord or rental group that is not affiliated with the university. Depending on the college, off-campus housing can range from extremely popular to non-existent. Students who choose to live off campus are typically given more freedom, but they also have to deal with possible subletting scenarios, furniture, bills, and other issues. In addition to these factors, rental prices and distance often affect a student's decision to move off campus.

**Office Hours** – Time that teachers set aside for students who have questions about coursework. Office hours are a good forum for students to go over any problems and to show interest in the subject material.

**Pledging** – The early phase of joining a fraternity or sorority, pledging takes place after a student has gone through rush and received a bid. Pledging usually lasts between one and two semesters. Once the pledging period is complete and a particular student has done everything that is required to become a member, that student is considered a brother or sister. If a fraternity or a sorority would decide to "haze" a group of students, this initiation would take place during the pledging period.

**Private Institution** – A school that does not use tax revenue to subsidize education costs. Private schools typically cost more than public schools and are usually smaller.

**Prof** – Slang for "professor."

**Public Institution** – A school that uses tax revenue to subsidize education costs. Public schools are often a good value for in-state residents and tend to be larger than most private colleges.

**Quarter System** (or Trimester System) – A type of academic calendar system. In this setup, students take classes for three academic periods. The first quarter usually starts in late September or early October and concludes right before Christmas. The second quarter usually starts around early to mid–January and finishes up around March or April. The last academic quarter, or "third quarter," usually starts in late March or early April and finishes up in late May or Mid-June. The fourth quarter is summer. The major difference between the quarter system and semester system is that students take more, less comprehensive courses under the quarter calendar.

**RA** (Resident Assistant) – A student leader who is assigned to a particular floor in a dormitory in order to help to the other students who live there. An RA's duties include ensuring student safety and providing assistance wherever possible.

**Recitation** – An extension of a specific course; a review session. Some classes, particularly large lectures, are supplemented with mandatory recitation sessions that provide a relatively personal class setting.

**Rolling Admissions** – A form of admissions. Most commonly found at public institutions, schools with this type of policy continue to accept students throughout the year until their class sizes are met. For example, some schools begin accepting students as early as December and will continue to do so until April or May.

**Room and Board** – This figure is typically the combined cost of a university-owned room and a meal plan.

**Room Draw/Housing Lottery** – A common way to pick on-campus room assignments for the following year. If a student decides to remain in university-owned housing, he or she is assigned a unique number that, along with seniority, is used to determine his or her housing for the next year.

**Rush** – The period in which students can meet the brothers and sisters of a particular chapter and find out if a given fraternity or sorority is right for them. Rushing a fraternity or a sorority is not a requirement at any school. The goal of rush is to give students who are serious about pledging a feel for what to expect.

**Semester System** – The most common type of academic calendar system at college campuses. This setup typically includes two semesters in a given school year. The fall semester starts around the end of August or early September and concludes before winter vacation. The spring semester usually starts in mid-January and ends in late April or May.

**Student Center/Rec Center/Student Union** – A common area on campus that often contains study areas, recreation facilities, and eateries. This building is often a good place to meet up with fellow students; depending on the school, the student center can have a huge role or a non-existent role in campus life.

**Student ID** – A university-issued photo ID that serves as a student's key to school-related functions. Some schools require students to show these cards in order to get into dorms, libraries, cafeterias, and other facilities. In addition to storing meal plan information, in some cases, a student ID can actually work as a debit card and allow students to purchase things from bookstores or local shops.

**Suite** – A type of dorm room. Unlike dorms that feature communal bathrooms shared by the entire floor, suites offer bathrooms shared only among the suite. Suite-style dorm rooms can house anywhere from two to ten students.

**TA** (Teacher's Assistant) – An undergraduate or grad student who helps in some manner with a specific course. In some cases, a TA will teach a class, assist a professor, grade assignments, or conduct office hours.

**Undergraduate** – A student in the process of studying for his or her bachelor's degree.

## ABOUT THE AUTHOR

I had a great time writing this book! I've just returned from a semester in Madrid, and it was really exciting to be able to delve into the world of Tufts all over again. I'm hoping that this will help me progress as a writer. I'm now a senior at Tufts University, pursuing degrees in both International Relations and Economics, while serving on the executive board of the *Tufts Daily*. I hope to use everything I've learned to work in business reporting in the future. Being from Philadelphia, Boston took a little getting used to, but now I know how to say "artery" like "ahtehy," and going to Tufts has been a wonderful experience. I hope this book has been insightful for you, and I hope you learned what it was really like to live "on the hill."

I'd like to give many people many thanks for supporting me while I attempted to work on this book. Thank you Mom, Dad, Alex, Grandma, George, Erika, Jon, Nick, Emily, Josh, Leah, Nico, Andrea, Naushin, Rachel, and everyone at College Prowler!

Emily Chasan
emilychasan@collegeprowler.com

# The College Prowler
# Big Book of Colleges

**Having Trouble Narrowing Down Your Choices?**
## Try Going Bigger!

BIG BOOK OF COLLEGES '09
7¼" X 10", 1248 Pages Paperback
$29.95 Retail
978-1-4274-0005-5

Choosing the perfect school can be an overwhelming
challenge. Luckily, our *Big Book of Colleges* makes
that task a little less daunting. We've packed it with
overviews of our full library of single-school guides—
more than 280 of the nation's top schools—giving you
some much-needed perspective on your search.

# College Prowler
# on the Web

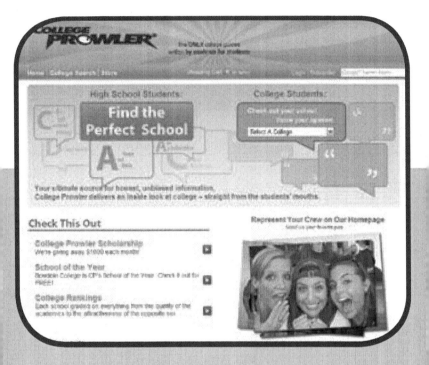

Craving some electronic interaction? Check out the new and improved **CollegeProwler.com**! We've included the COMPLETE contents of more than 250 of our single-school guides on the Web—and you can gain access to all of them for just $39.95 per year!

Not only that, but non-subscribers can still view and compare our grades for each school, order books at our online bookstore, or enter our monthly scholarship contest. Don't get left in the dark when making your college decision. Let College Prowler be your guide!

# Get the Jolt!

## *College Jolt gives you a peek behind the scenes*

College Jolt is our new blog designed to hook you up with great information, funny videos, cool contests, awesome scholarship opportunities, and honest insight into who we are and what we're all about.

Check us out at *www.collegejolt.com*

# Tell Us What Life Is Really Like at Your School!

Have you ever wanted to let people know what your college is really like? Now's your chance to help millions of high school students choose the right college.

## Let your voice be heard.

Check out *www.collegeprowler.com* for more info!

# Need More Help?

Do you have more questions about this school? Can't find a certain statistic? College Prowler is here to help. We are the best source of college information out there. We have a network of thousands of students who can get the latest information on any school to you ASAP. E-mail us at info@collegeprowler.com with your college-related questions.

**E-Mail Us Your College-Related Questions!**

Check out *www.collegeprowler.com* for more details.
1-800-290-2682

# Write For Us!
## *Get published! Voice your opinion.*

Writing a College Prowler guidebook is both fun and rewarding; our open-ended format allows your own creativity free reign. Our writers have been featured in national newspapers and have seen their names in bookstores across the country. Now is your chance to break into the publishing industry with one of the country's fastest-growing publishers!

Apply now at **www.collegeprowler.com**

Contact editor@collegeprowler.com or call 1-800-290-2682 for more details.

# Pros and Cons

Still can't figure out if this is the right school for you?
You've already read through this in-depth guide;
why not list the pros and cons? It will really help
with narrowing down your decision and determining
whether or not this school is right for you.

| Pros | Cons |
|------|------|
| ..................................... | ..................................... |
| ..................................... | ..................................... |
| ..................................... | ..................................... |
| ..................................... | ..................................... |
| ..................................... | ..................................... |
| ..................................... | ..................................... |
| ..................................... | ..................................... |
| ..................................... | ..................................... |
| ..................................... | ..................................... |
| ..................................... | ..................................... |
| ..................................... | ..................................... |
| ..................................... | ..................................... |
| ..................................... | ..................................... |

# Pros and Cons

Still can't figure out if this is the right school for you?
You've already read through this in-depth guide;
why not list the pros and cons? It will really help
with narrowing down your decision and determining
whether or not this school is right for you.

| Pros | Cons |
|------|------|
| ..................................... | ..................................... |
| ..................................... | ..................................... |
| ..................................... | ..................................... |
| ..................................... | ..................................... |
| ..................................... | ..................................... |
| ..................................... | ..................................... |
| ..................................... | ..................................... |
| ..................................... | ..................................... |
| ..................................... | ..................................... |
| ..................................... | ..................................... |
| ..................................... | ..................................... |
| ..................................... | ..................................... |
| ..................................... | ..................................... |

# Notes

..................................................................

..................................................................

..................................................................

..................................................................

..................................................................

..................................................................

..................................................................

..................................................................

..................................................................

..................................................................

..................................................................

..................................................................

..................................................................

..................................................................

# Notes

....................................................................

....................................................................

....................................................................

....................................................................

....................................................................

....................................................................

....................................................................

....................................................................

....................................................................

....................................................................

....................................................................

....................................................................

....................................................................

# Notes

......................................................................

......................................................................

......................................................................

......................................................................

......................................................................

......................................................................

......................................................................

......................................................................

......................................................................

......................................................................

......................................................................

......................................................................

......................................................................

# Notes

...................................................................

...................................................................

...................................................................

...................................................................

...................................................................

...................................................................

...................................................................

...................................................................

...................................................................

...................................................................

...................................................................

...................................................................

...................................................................

...................................................................

# Notes

........................................................

........................................................

........................................................

........................................................

........................................................

........................................................

........................................................

........................................................

........................................................

........................................................

........................................................

........................................................

........................................................

# Notes

........................................................

........................................................

........................................................

........................................................

........................................................

........................................................

........................................................

........................................................

........................................................

........................................................

........................................................

........................................................

........................................................

# Notes

..................................................................

..................................................................

..................................................................

..................................................................

..................................................................

..................................................................

..................................................................

..................................................................

..................................................................

..................................................................

..................................................................

..................................................................

..................................................................

# Notes

....................................................................

....................................................................

....................................................................

....................................................................

....................................................................

....................................................................

....................................................................

....................................................................

....................................................................

....................................................................

....................................................................

....................................................................

....................................................................

# Notes

....................................................................

....................................................................

....................................................................

....................................................................

....................................................................

....................................................................

....................................................................

....................................................................

....................................................................

....................................................................

....................................................................

....................................................................

....................................................................

# Notes

....................................................................

....................................................................

....................................................................

....................................................................

....................................................................

....................................................................

....................................................................

....................................................................

....................................................................

....................................................................

....................................................................

....................................................................

....................................................................

# Notes

....................................................................

....................................................................

....................................................................

....................................................................

....................................................................

....................................................................

....................................................................

....................................................................

....................................................................

....................................................................

....................................................................

....................................................................

....................................................................

# Notes

..............................................................................

..............................................................................

..............................................................................

..............................................................................

..............................................................................

..............................................................................

..............................................................................

..............................................................................

..............................................................................

..............................................................................

..............................................................................

..............................................................................

..............................................................................

# Notes

......................................................

......................................................

......................................................

......................................................

......................................................

......................................................

......................................................

......................................................

......................................................

......................................................

......................................................

......................................................

......................................................

# Notes

.................................................................

.................................................................

.................................................................

.................................................................

.................................................................

.................................................................

.................................................................

.................................................................

.................................................................

.................................................................

.................................................................

.................................................................

.................................................................

**COLLEGE PROWLER®**

| | | | |
|---|---|---|---|
| Albion College | Franklin & Marshall College | Ohio State University | University of Colorado |
| Alfred University | Furman University | Ohio University | University of Connecticut |
| Allegheny College | Geneva College | Ohio Wesleyan University | University of Delaware |
| American University | George Washington University | Old Dominion University | University of Denver |
| Amherst College | Georgetown University | Penn State University | University of Florida |
| Arizona State University | Georgia Tech | Pepperdine University | University of Georgia |
| Auburn University | Gettysburg College | Pitzer College | University of Illinois |
| Babson College | Gonzaga University | Pomona College | University of Iowa |
| Ball State University | Goucher College | Princeton University | University of Kansas |
| Bard College | Grinnell College | Providence College | University of Kentucky |
| Barnard College | Grove City College | Purdue University | University of Maine |
| Bates College | Guilford College | Reed College | University of Maryland |
| Baylor University | Gustavus Adolphus College | Rensselaer Polytechnic Institute | University of Massachusetts |
| Beloit College | Hamilton College | Rhode Island School of Design | University of Miami |
| Bentley College | Hampshire College | Rhodes College | University of Michigan |
| Binghamton University | Hampton University | Rice University | University of Minnesota |
| Birmingham Southern College | Hanover College | Rochester Institute of Technology | University of Mississippi |
| Boston College | Harvard University | Rollins College | University of Missouri |
| Boston University | Harvey Mudd College | Rutgers University | University of Nebraska |
| Bowdoin College | Haverford College | San Diego State University | University of New Hampshire |
| Brandeis University | Hofstra University | Santa Clara University | University of North Carolina |
| Brigham Young University | Hollins University | Sarah Lawrence College | University of Notre Dame |
| Brown University | Howard University | Scripps College | University of Oklahoma |
| Bryn Mawr College | Idaho State University | Seattle University | University of Oregon |
| Bucknell University | Illinois State University | Seton Hall University | University of Pennsylvania |
| Cal Poly | Illinois Wesleyan University | Simmons College | University of Pittsburgh |
| Cal Poly Pomona | Indiana University | Skidmore College | University of Puget Sound |
| Cal State Northridge | Iowa State University | Slippery Rock | University of Rhode Island |
| Cal State Sacramento | Ithaca College | Smith College | University of Richmond |
| Caltech | IUPUI | Southern Methodist University | University of Rochester |
| Carleton College | James Madison University | Southwestern University | University of San Diego |
| Carnegie Mellon University | Johns Hopkins University | Spelman College | University of San Francisco |
| Case Western Reserve | Juniata College | St. Joseph's University Philladelphia | University of South Carolina |
| Centenary College of Louisiana | Kansas State | St. John's University | University of South Dakota |
| Centre College | Kent State University | St. Louis University | University of South Florida |
| Claremont McKenna College | Kenyon College | St. Olaf College | University of Southern California |
| Clark Atlanta University | Lafayette College | Stanford University | University of Tennessee |
| Clark University | LaRoche College | Stetson University | University of Texas |
| Clemson University | Lawrence University | Stony Brook University | University of Utah |
| Colby College | Lehigh University | Susquhanna University | University of Vermont |
| Colgate University | Lewis & Clark College | Swarthmore College | University of Virginia |
| College of Charleston | Louisiana State University | Syracuse University | University of Washington |
| College of the Holy Cross | Loyola College in Maryland | Temple University | University of Wisconsin |
| College of William & Mary | Loyola Marymount University | Tennessee State University | UNLV |
| College of Wooster | Loyola University Chicago | Texas A & M University | Ursinus College |
| Colorado College | Loyola University New Orleans | Texas Christian University | Valparaiso University |
| Columbia University | Macalester College | Towson University | Vanderbilt University |
| Connecticut College | Marlboro College | Trinity College Connecticut | Vassar College |
| Cornell University | Marquette University | Trinity University Texas | Villanova University |
| Creighton University | McGill University | Truman State | Virginia Tech |
| CUNY Hunters College | Miami University of Ohio | Tufts University | Wake Forest University |
| Dartmouth College | Michigan State University | Tulane University | Warren Wilson College |
| Davidson College | Middle Tennessee State | UC Berkeley | Washington and Lee University |
| Denison University | Middlebury College | UC Davis | Washington University in St. Louis |
| DePauw University | Millsaps College | UC Irvine | Wellesley College |
| Dickinson College | MIT | UC Riverside | Wesleyan University |
| Drexel University | Montana State University | UC San Diego | West Point |
| Duke University | Mount Holyoke College | UC Santa Barbara | West Virginia University |
| Duquesne University | Muhlenberg College | UC Santa Cruz | Wheaton College IL |
| Earlham College | New York University | UCLA | Wheaton College MA |
| East Carolina University | North Carolina State | Union College | Whitman College |
| Elon University | Northeastern University | University at Albany | Wilkes University |
| Emerson College | Northern Arizona University | University at Buffalo | Williams College |
| Emory University | Northern Illinois University | University of Alabama | Xavier University |
| FIT | Northwestern University | University of Arizona | Yale University |
| Florida State University | Oberlin College | University of Central Florida | |
| Fordham University | Occidental College | University of Chicago | |

Made in the USA
Lexington, KY
24 June 2010